POOLS OF GRACE

ON BEING A CONTEMPLATIVE CHURCH

Recent years have seen a renewal of contemplative practice in Western Christianity, yet this renewal has not necessarily permeated the ethos and practice of regular worshiping communities. Many parishes or congregations have a meditation group as one of their activities, but few local churches allow for a liturgy shaped and undergirded by contemplative silence in their main gathering for worship, and fewer still are committed to contemplative practice suffusing the whole of their life together and their service in the world.

Benedictus Contemplative Church is an ecumenical Christian community with a practice of contemplation at its heart. Founded in 2012, Benedictus has been exploring the gift and call of contemplative church for our time. This series offers reflections and resources grounded in the Benedictus experience that we hope may contribute to the continued emergence of contemplative forms of church.

Series Editor
Heather Thomson

POOLS OF GRACE

The Gift and Call of Contemplative Worship

Sarah Bachelard

WIPF & STOCK · Eugene, Oregon

POOLS OF GRACE
The Gift and Call of Contemplative Worship

On Being a Contemplative Church Series

Copyright © 2026 Sarah Bachelard. All rights reserved. Except for brief quotations in critical publications or reviews, no part of this book may be reproduced in any manner without prior written permission from the publisher. Write: Permissions, Wipf and Stock Publishers, 199 W. 8th Ave., Suite 3, Eugene, OR 97401.

Wipf & Stock
An Imprint of Wipf and Stock Publishers
199 W. 8th Ave., Suite 3
Eugene, OR 97401

www.wipfandstock.com

PAPERBACK ISBN: 979-8-3852-3057-0
HARDCOVER ISBN: 979-8-3852-3058-7
EBOOK ISBN: 979-8-3852-3059-4

VERSION NUMBER 01/06/26

Permissions

Grateful acknowledgment is given for permission to print from the following sources:

David Adam, *Tides and Seasons: Modern Prayers in the Celtic Tradition* © David Adam 1989. London: SPCK, 1989. Reproduced with permission from the Licensor through PLSclear.

Scripture quotations are from New Revised Standard Version Bible, copyright © 1989 National Council of the Churches of Christ in the United States of America. Used by permission. All rights reserved worldwide.

Photographs are by members of the Benedictus Contemplative Photography group, and used by permission.
Susanna Pain, "Different Perspectives"
Neil Millar, "Turn to Wonder"
Kate Smith, "Mystery River"
Frances Marston, "Shadow Shell"
Neil Millar, "Entering In"

*Dedicated to the members of Benedictus Contemplative Church
and to emerging contemplative communities everywhere.*

CONTENTS

Series Foreword | xi
Acknowledgments | xv

1 The Being of Contemplative Church | 1
2 Approaching Contemplative Worship | 24
3 Shaping Contemplative Liturgy | 39
4 Creating Contemplative Liturgy: A Reflection on Practice | 73
   JENNY STEWART
5 Integrating Worship | 82

Bibliography | 105

SERIES FOREWORD

> "Let anyone who has an ear listen to what
> the Spirit is saying to the churches."
>
> —REVELATION 2:29

> Listen, my children, to your master's precepts,
> and incline the ear of your heart.
>
> —RULE OF ST. BENEDICT

> Christian life is a listening life.
>
> —ROWAN WILLIAMS

THESE ARE QUOTATIONS FROM the Revelation to St. John, the Rule of Benedict, and contemporary theologian Rowan Williams. They are a tiny sampling of the countless exhortations to "listen" that animate the Christian tradition. Each assumes there is something or someone to listen to, that there is communication coming towards us, inviting our hearing, our response. They thus suggest that Christianity is essentially an answering faith. It arises as recognition of and response to the prior reality of God and calls us always to increasingly self-forgetful, self-emptying adoration. "You did not choose me but I chose you," said Jesus to his disciples (John 15:16).

From this perspective, to speak of *contemplative* Christianity or *contemplative* church is tautological—as if there could be any authentic Christianity or church that is not contemplative, not essentially attentive and responsive to Another. And yet, in the worship and common life of many Christian communities, an understanding of this intrinsically contemplative dimension of faith can be muted, neglected, or even lost altogether. For all the talk of listening for and waiting on God, Christianity can become little more than a system of ideas to adhere to, an activity to perform. The reason this happens, I suggest, is that without a disciplined *practice* of contemplation, we forget what the tradition is really talking about. There is no formation of capacity to listen at sufficient depth, no learning to behold with the eye of the heart. Thus, the church becomes less and less capable of communicating as living truth the transfiguring receptivity to the mind of Christ in which it is sourced.

In recent decades, in the Western church, there has been a revival of the teaching and practice of Christian contemplative prayer. Communities such as Contemplative Outreach and the World Community for Christian Meditation have reminded the church of its own contemplative roots and heart. Renewed access to these roots has deepened the faith of many and offered others a way back into vital engagement with a tradition they believed they had left behind. Yet this contemplative renewal of Christian faith has not necessarily permeated the ethos and practice of regular worshiping communities. Though some parishes or congregations have a meditation group as one of their activities or offerings, fewer allow for a liturgy shaped and undergirded by contemplative silence in their main service, and fewer still are committed to a contemplative approach suffusing the whole of their life together.

In 2012, I was part of founding Benedictus Contemplative Church. We are an ecumenical community committed to being a contemplative church in this fuller sense. Two years after we began, I asked Father Laurence Freeman, director of the World Community for Christian Meditation, to reflect on the offering Benedictus sought to be. His words still, for me, evoke the heart of our calling. He wrote, "Benedictus strikes me as a fresh, refreshing and contemporary manifestation of Christian faith and community for our time. Benedictus brings the depth dimension of contemplative spirituality into the experience of both worship and fellowship. . . . It is not only the church that benefits from this. The social institutions with which the church works in the world are also challenged to live at a level beyond outward appearance and to make compassion and wisdom integral to their vision and way of life."[1]

In recent years, we have been contacted by people from all over Australia and beyond who want to know if there is something like Benedictus where they live. Likewise, we are contacted regularly by congregational leaders and chaplains, ordained and lay, who feel drawn to initiate something along these lines. From Argentina, Belgium, Ireland, the United States, the United Kingdom, and Australia, it seems there is a sense of something needed and seeking a way. What seems significant is that these inquiries and conversations are not driven by a desire to "save" the institutional church or restore Christianity's lost cultural power and prestige. Rather, they emerge from a yearning for forms of gathering and prayer capable of connecting more deeply to the truth of God and to contemporary contexts and need.

This series aims to share aspects of the Benedictus experience and practice. Ours is not the only model for being a contemplative church, but it is an expression that has persisted over time and serves the needs of a large and geographically dispersed community. Our hope is that in offering reflections on and resources from our life together, some of the possibilities and challenges presented by other contexts might come into focus. We seek thus to contribute to the emergence of Christian contemplative worshiping communities capable of listening deeply and responding courageously to the call of God in our time.

Sarah Bachelard

1. Laurence Freeman, testimonial on the Benedictus Contemplative Church website, benedictus.com.au.

ACKNOWLEDGMENTS

MY MOTHER LIKES TO tell the story of the origins of Benedictus like this. "She just came home one day and said, 'Mum, I'm going to start a church.' And she did." This has the advantage of dramatic simplicity but, as well as missing the backstory, it obscures the essentially communal foundations of our life together.

It is true that, from the beginning, I have been the designated leader of Benedictus Contemplative Church and taken primary responsibility for enabling our worship and other gatherings. Contemplative prayer, silent meditation, have been at the heart of my own Christian practice for many years and I was inspired by the possibility of allowing this kind of prayer to shape the whole of a congregation's life. But the original idea for initiating an ecumenical contemplative worshiping community came from my partner, Reverend Dr. Neil Millar. His was the initial inspiration, and the essential ethos and form of Benedictus began to emerge first in our conversations.

The possibility of Benedictus took further steps towards becoming incarnate when Neil and I shared our emerging vision with our friends Reverend Susanna Pain and her husband Reverend Dr. Nikolai Blaskow. At that time, Susanna was the rector of an Anglican parish in Canberra and, as well as helping us discern and refine our vision for Benedictus, she provided the necessary practical support in the form of a place to meet, insurance coverage, and a canopy under which the Benedictus seedling could take root and begin to grow. We were always clear that Benedictus was a

Acknowledgments

separate entity, not an offering of the parish itself. But the hospitality, encouragement, and advocacy of Susanna, Nikolai, and many of the parishioners of Holy Covenant were profoundly significant in enabling us to happen. Their support continues, with Susanna now working with Benedictus and Nikolai contributing in a range of ways.

Another early and important supporter was Father Laurence Freeman, director of the World Community for Christian Meditation. Although the idea of Benedictus emerged at a time of great turmoil and transition for me, Laurence caught its spirit immediately. By giving us his blessing, he not only encouraged us to trust where we were being led, but helped to give legitimacy to our enterprise. And then there were those who first attended and participated, contributing their prayer and listening, their musical and organizational gifts, and their financial support as we began gently to form as a community. Gradually Benedictus grew. Through our website and through my writing and teaching in other contexts, we have always had connections with people beyond Canberra. When our weekly service became available online during the COVID-19 pandemic in 2020 and 2021, we became suddenly accessible to a much wider range of people. We now have members who attend regularly in person and online from around Australia and around the world, enabling us to extend our offerings further.

This series, On Being a Contemplative Church, emerges from this journey and the many who have participated in it. I am especially grateful to Dr. Heather Thomson, theologian and founding member of the Benedictus Liturgy Group, who first conceived of sharing our experience this way, and who will be our series editor. I offer my thanks also to another member of the Benedictus Liturgy Group, Dr. Jenny Stewart, who has worked with Heather and me to shape this first book in the series and contributed her reflections on the process of creating liturgy in chapter 4. Over the years, the liturgy group has had a number of different members. For their generosity and creativity in writing or shaping the

Acknowledgments

original liturgies shared here, I gratefully acknowledge also Meryl Turner, Sarah Legrand, Valerie Albrecht, Deb May, Hazel Hunt, and Paul Hartigan.

— 1 —

THE BEING OF CONTEMPLATIVE CHURCH

"We're collectively living a life that no longer exists."[1] In these words, English philosopher Jonathan Rowson finds a powerful expression of the lived experience of our age. Though for many of us the climate crisis looms largest in our fears and imaginations, Rowson sees this as but one aspect of a crisis that also encompasses "democratic deconsolidation, widespread economic precarity, intergenerational injustice, race relations, cultural polarization and loneliness or depression."[2] In a similar vein, Jem Bendell has identified the many facets of a "societal collapse" already underway that, he argues, encompasses the biosphere and monetary, economic, energy, and food systems.[3]

All this is crisis enough, but it is accompanied, both Rowson and Bendell suggest, by an overarching crisis of knowledge and action. Despite our capacity to recognize and name (at least to some extent) the interlocking and terrifying trends in which we are all caught, our capacity to know how to be or act in response seems radically incommensurate with the urgency of the situation. Rowson writes: "Most people still appear to be running on autopilot

---

1. The words are from Ivo Mensch, cited by Rowson, *Metamodernity*, 17.
2. Rowson, *Metamodernity*, 18.
3. Bendell, *Breaking Together*, 24.

with an outdated kind of fuel, drunk on ideas of progress, our own significance and the notion that things will somehow be OK."[4] And even if we have woken up, it is not at all clear what any of us can do; even how we conceive of or imagine our situation is up for grabs. "All of our rallying cries for action and for transformation arise in cultures and psyches riddled with confusion and immunities to change," says Rowson. "We have to better understand *who* and *what* we are, individually and collectively, in order to be able to fundamentally change *how* we act. That conundrum is what is now widely called the meta-crisis lying within, between and beyond . . . the crisis."[5] Or, as he also says, we live in "a time between worlds," where the spiritual and material exhaustion of modernity is becoming ever more clear,[6] but new ways of seeing, being, and acting are yet to emerge at scale.

I am not going to suggest that a few local contemplative Christian communities are the answer to all this. At the same time, it does seem that awareness (even implicit awareness) of the "material and spiritual exhaustion of modernity" is part of what is opening many of our contemporaries to a hunger for something like contemplation, for something deeper and more real than "the insane world that our financial systems and our advertising culture and our chaotic and unexamined emotions encourage us to inhabit."[7] A contemplative church, then, is not just one that happens to practice meditation; it is growing in ways of knowing and being that connect us more truly to reality and is thus capable of speaking to some of the transformation of persons and cultures that seems required. For this reason, before we enter directly into the question of contemplative forms and expressions of church, I want to say more to situate its emergence in this larger context.

---

4. Rowson, *Metamodernity*, 17.
5. Rowson, *Metamodernity*, 29.
6. Rowson, *Metamodernity*, 30.
7. Williams, "Address to the Synod," para. 8.

The Being of Contemplative Church

CONTEXT AND EMERGENCE

Let me draw out briefly three interrelated aspects of our situation. The first involves the need to recover a sense of ourselves as part of a whole, or as St. Paul puts it, our awareness of being "members one of another" (Rom 12:5), and of the whole earth community. At one level, the fact that we are profoundly interdependent is a truism. A moment's reflection tells us that we are born into a world, a culture, and a network of conversations that massively precede us, and in relationship with which we are dependent for everything we are and might be—for our embodiment and physical survival, as well as for language, identity, consciousness, and meaning.

And yet, though most people may be prepared to assent to this truth in the abstract and in general, it is quite another matter to realize it in the way we live. Especially in modern Western culture, we seem so often separated from a felt sense of our belonging with, to, and for the whole. Concerning our separation from the natural world, environmental philosophers point to the persistent anthropocentrism of Western thought, which is sourced in a dualism that "set the human apart from and above nature."[8] Concerning our separation from one another and from the sense of participating in and being answerable to a larger web of relationship, religious thinkers point to the related tendency to seek for self-sufficiency and the illusion of autonomy. So what is the difference between knowing *about* our interconnectedness and realizing it in practice, such that this knowledge actually makes a difference to how we live in the world?

Rowson points to the shift that happened for some, at least, during the COVID-19 pandemic. Writing in the aftermath of that experience, he noted: "Many events, processes and things in the world that *are* objectively real can only *become* real within us or between us when we are directly implicated in that process of becoming. On this reading, the COVID-19 pandemic means that the systemic fragility of a planetary civilization that was already real just *became real* for millions of people. Our shared mortality,

---

8. Mathews, *Dao of Civilization*, 16.

biological inheritance and ecological interdependence became real. The vulnerability of our food, water and energy supplies became real. The deluded nature of plutocratic, extractive, surveillance capitalism became real. The value of care-based relationships and professions, and the solidarity of strangers became real."[9]

In other words, what may enable many of us fully to *realize* our interdependence, and the futility of systems and forms of life that deny it, is the lived experience of fragility, the breakdown of illusions of autonomy and mastery, such as occurred during the global pandemic and can also happen in times of natural disaster, war, and political persecution, as well as in more quotidian experiences of aging, illness, failure, and grief. And yet, we do not *have* to wait for disaster to strike. Some forms of life recognize and sustain this awareness organically and habitually. For example, through ceremony, song, story, and material practices, many pre-agrarian and indigenous cultures engender a habitual sense of embeddedness in and answerability to the whole. They practice an intentional reverencing of interdependence that allows for the regeneration and flourishing of life and a very different vision of the human vocation than is offered by extractive capitalism.

Contemplative practice can also enable an opening to the felt sense of fuller belonging and answerability. In wordless, imageless prayer, we practice letting go the stream of thoughts and feelings that constitute our sense of separateness. We seek to be simply open, receptive to the presence and pattern of the basic energy of reality. The Christian tradition has tended to emphasize the effect of this practice in terms of being restored to connection with ourselves, other people, and God.[10] I know I am not alone, however, in discovering that what also comes alive through contemplative practice is a much deeper sense of connection with the natural world. As we are liberated from self-absorption and self-concern, we become more aware of the greater life around us—the presence of a tree, the quickness of a bird or insect, the touch of wind and water, the immensity of sky. Contemplative practice helps us

---

9. Rowson, *Metamodernity*, 24.
10. Main, *Monastery Without Walls*, 50.

become more fully present and alive to the wonder of what is. It increases our sense of belonging to a larger whole and our reverence for its mysterious otherness. Importantly, this is not just about how we feel; it is about how and what we may know. It is about the renewing of our mind and the expanding of our intelligence.

This brings me to the second aspect of our situation I want to highlight. The problem with a dualistic worldview is not only that it falsely separates us from the larger life of which we are part, encouraging attitudes of alienation and exploitation. The further and related problem is that it distorts and limits our capacity for truthfully apprehending the fullness of reality and hence for learning how we might go on in relationship to it. How so? The main issue is the extent to which dualistic reasoning tends to limit us to knowing things "from the outside," and thus to being alienated from the "inner life" of the world. Rather than entering embodied relationship, learning to know through participation in and receptivity to what is given, the dualistically minded modern subject tends to be distanced from the world, sometimes standing over against it.

In his rich and illuminating discussion of the thought of Evagrius in this regard, Rowan Williams identifies the key difference here in terms of the active and contemplative dispositions. Williams suggests that knowledge "from the outside" involves the human subject actively seeking to generate knowledge by applying her own ideas "as potential tools for making intelligible connections between phenomena and representing them accordingly."[11] This is an important human capacity and there is nothing wrong with it per se. There is, however, always a risk that, when corrupted by an aggressive or acquisitive spirit, this way of knowing the world becomes a search for merely instrumental or "technical mastery."[12] It can tend to reduce the world to serving the interests of those who have gained such supposed knowledge of it.

For Evagrius, however, true knowledge is far richer than this knowledge from the outside. It involves tuning in to the deeper

---

11. Williams, *Looking East in Winter*, 64.
12. Williams, *Looking East in Winter*, 65.

energies and intelligible structure of the world, which participates in and reflects the intelligence of the Creator. This "tuning in" is a contemplative awareness[13]—a non-grasping, non-acquisitive opening to the fullness of reality, by means of which "the mind is opened to the unifying source" of every existent thing, the Logos or "self-communication of God."[14] There seems to be a striking parallel between Evagrius's understanding and the account of indigenous ways of knowing offered by Australian First Nations scholar Tyson Yunkaporta. Yunkaporta writes that from an indigenous perspective, "the whole is intelligent, and each part carries the inherent intelligence of the whole system. Knowledge is therefore a living thing that is patterned within every person and being and object and phenomenon within creation."[15] He likewise connects the possibility of knowing the world at this level to a contemplative disposition. "Respectful observation and interaction within the system, with the parts and the connections between them, is the only way to see the pattern. You cannot know any part, let alone the whole, without respect. You cannot come to knowledge without it."[16]

I think we can readily see the difference in these two ways of knowing when we think of how we may relate to one another. There is a vast difference between seeing other people as bundles of properties and reactions with a value connected primarily to what they can do for me, and seeing them as persons with an inner life of their own, with a depth and integrity not simply meant for my scrutiny or use.[17] In our culture, we are generally less practiced at beholding this "innerness" in the other-than-human world. Yet Williams goes on: "A world whose sanity is restored would be

13. Williams, *Looking East in Winter*, 67.
14. Williams, *Looking East in Winter*, 68.
15. Yunkaporta, *Sand Talk*, 95.
16. Yunkaporta, *Sand Talk*, 95. Maggie Ross also notes the significance of the concept of respect in indigenous cultures and relates it to contemplative consciousness: "Respect is life: respect for the signals the environment is sending; respect for silence; respect for the wisdom of elders; respect for one's own acuity; even respect for failings" (Ross, *Silence*, 224).
17. Cf. Williams, "Address to the Synod," para. 10.

one in which 'reason' had been rediscovered as a condition not [merely] of instrumental control and conceptual precision but of *appropriate responsiveness*, to the human and the non-human order alike."[18] He quotes Flannery O'Connor lamenting the way in which this fuller conception of reason has "lost ground" in modernity because of the way grace and nature, imagination and reason have been separated. What an artist does, she writes, is to use his reason "to discover an answering reason in everything he sees. For him, *to be reasonable is to find in the object, in the situation, in the sequence, the spirit which makes it itself.*"[19]

The difficulty is that to transform our way of knowing in this regard is not something we can just decide to do. It is a fruit of certain kinds of practice. Williams notes that the *truly* knowing human subject shares "in a network of embodied interactions, which it attends to, learns from and takes time with."[20] Australian First Nations peoples speak of such things as "walking on country" and of deep listening, or *dadirri*.[21] For Evagrius, this kind of awareness or intelligence is cultivated by practices that liberate the knower from self-centered habits of mind that "reduce" or "de-realize" the world because they encourage us to "see" only in terms of our wants and needs.[22] Such practices include hospitality and generosity, as well as contemplative forms of prayer.

On this account, to grow in wisdom and knowledge is not just about accumulating information, or sharpening a narrow set of critical tools in logic and argument. It involves spiritual practice that liberates thought from habits of aggression and acquisition,

---

18. Williams, *Looking East in Winter*, 69; emphasis original.
19. Williams, *Looking East in Winter*, 77; emphasis original.
20. Williams, *Looking East in Winter*, 67.
21. See Mathews, *Dao of Civilization*, 61. "Dadirri" is a practice of "deep listening and quiet, still awareness" known by the Daly River people of the Northern Territory and taught by Miriam Rose Ungunmerr (Ungunmerr, "Dadirri"). Stan Grant notes that, for Wiradjiri people in western NSW, "Yindyamarra" denotes the same kind of understanding, "a space of quiet, peace and kindness . . . a traditional space of reciprocity that forms a cornerstone of our existence" (Grant, *Murriyang*, 28).
22. Williams, *Looking East in Winter*, 66.

so as to expand the capacity of mind to receive the fullness of what is given. Mark Vernon understands what he calls "spiritual intelligence" as growing with "a concern for rituals, worship and the arts, alongside reason, rules and the sciences." Such activities, he says, "can align individuals and groups to deeper pulses of reality and carry them to the shorelines of knowledge, where learning becomes a type of listening, thought a type of resonance, and personal change a type of inner expansion."[23]

So, let me summarize briefly. I have been aiming to situate my reflections on the gift and call of contemplative church in the broader context of our time, and have sought to identify aspects of the transformation of our culture and ourselves that seem required if we are to become capable of responding at anything like the right level. I have spoken of the need to recover a lived sense of our belonging and answerability to the whole, and connected this with the restoration of our sanity. For sanity implies the capacity truly to apprehend the reality of which we are part and so to reason about and relate to it in ways that lead not to continued destruction but to life. Recall Rowson saying that "we have to better understand *who* and *what* we are, individually and collectively, in order to be able to fundamentally change *how* we act." I have suggested that contemplative consciousness and practice are at the heart of how we might begin to be more realistically in relation with the whole and form an intelligence adequate to the world itself. I have suggested that an implicit awareness of this need may be part of what is drawing more and more people to contemplative practice of various kinds.

I want, finally, to touch on a third aspect of the necessary transformation of our culture and society. It has to do with the formation of communities of practice that incarnate our common humanity and the sense of "us" or "we." "What should we do? How should we be?" To ask these questions, Jonathan Rowson points out, is to realize that "we don't have a viable We."[24] "Perhaps spiritually we are One," he writes, "but politically we are many." What

---

23. Vernon, "Spiritual Intelligence," 9.
24. Rowson, *Metamodernity*, 33.

this means, in the context of the climate and other crises, is that "the We that wants to say there is an emergency is not the same We as the We that needs to hear it, and the We that needs to hear it has several different ideas about the nature of the We that should do something about it."[25]

One response to this conundrum is to pose the question individualistically. What should I do? This is important in the sense that it requires each of us to be responsible for our participation in the web, accountable for offering our particular gifts, skills, and energies "to address what is most generatively helpful, and collaborate with other individuating people."[26] But the issues we face are not only individual; they are (as Rowson puts it) "collective action problems." To address them calls for some kind of collective response. He goes on: "While the kind of We that might actually be fit for purpose cannot be wished into existence, then it can perhaps be forged." Rowson describes this forging as "an educational process"—one that simultaneously enables each person to recognize and realize the part they have to play while generating a "collective sensibility," "a global commons, such that people *feel* their individual actions are a palpable part of a global web of life."[27] This We, constituted by maturing individuals, is what our predicament calls for—"a planetary-scale response that is both profoundly collective and deeply personal."[28]

When I first read this, I wrote in the margins of my copy of Rowson's essay "role of the church." This may seem grandiose and deluded. But then I ask myself, what is the church called to be if not a community that forges persons who are growing into the fullness of their own gift and call, while simultaneously learning who and how they are called to be for the sake of the whole? What is the church if not a community in the process of realizing a corporate identity capable of radically collaborative action, the body

---

25. Rowson, *Metamodernity*, 33.
26. Rowson, *Metamodernity*, 33.
27. Rowson, *Metamodernity*, 35.
28. Rowson, *Metamodernity*, 36.

of Christ, while never forgetting the uniqueness and lovability of each one, each sparrow and flower of the field?

We do not have a viable "We." But could a community deepening its responsiveness to the living Spirit and Word animating the whole life of the world, a community ever more contemplatively attuned to share in responsibility for the whole—could such a community begin to make visible what "We" might be? Could we be living as listeners to such an extent that we become something like the sacrament of a new society? A sign, as the church is always called to be, of God's truth becoming manifest in our midst, making visible the fullness of creaturely life to which all are called, and so part of forging a new creation amid the spiritual and material exhaustion of our age? This might seem an overblown rhetoric when we think of the small and fragile expressions of contemplative church currently emerging, and when we remember what seems the inexorable decline of the wider church in the West. Yet the fact remains, something is coming into being in the midst of both social and ecclesial collapse; new ways of being together are being evoked.

I am aware that beginning in this way may seem to put the cart before the horse. As if contemplation is first a "tool" for addressing our own needs, a remedy for our society's ills, rather than a way of prayer that leads us more deeply into the knowledge and love of God for its own sake. As if contemplative church is more about our agenda and corporate survival, than it is a response to God's prior reality and call. In fact, I do not think there is any necessary tension between these things.

In the Christian vision, the call of God is never to some isolated enclave, cut off from the rest of life. "A Christianity that withdraws from the world falls prey to unnaturalness, irrationality, triumphalism and arbitrariness," wrote Dietrich Bonhoeffer.[29] Because Christ has entered into the world, to love and reconcile the world, there is for his followers "nowhere to retreat from the world, neither externally nor into the inner life. . . . As reality is *one* in Christ, so the person who belongs to this Christ-reality is

---

29. Bonhoeffer, *Ethics*, 61.

also a whole. Worldliness does not separate one from Christ, and being Christian does not separate one from the world. Belonging completely to Christ, one stands at the same time completely in the world."[30]

Bonhoeffer summed up this line of thought brilliantly: the church is not a cult.[31] It does not exist for itself, but for the world; and Jesus Christ has to do not with some supposedly separate spiritual realm but with the whole of reality. The deeper our prayer, the greater our love and concern for the world. As St. John put it, "Those who say, 'I love God,' and hate their brothers and sisters, are liars" (1 John 4:20). Conversely, then, it is not surprising that the more we seek to engage with the truth and needs of the world, the more we encounter Christ's call and the leading of his Spirit into life. And this brings us to the point at which we may start to engage more directly with the gift and call of contemplative church.

THE NARROW GATE

What brings people to Benedictus, the contemplative church I lead? Some who come describe themselves as refugees from churches, even mainline churches, that they have experienced as operating more like "cults" (in Bonhoeffer's sense) than as belonging and accountable to the whole. Some, for example, have experienced the refusal of a Christian community to reckon honestly with questions of sexuality, gender identity, marital or personal breakdown, and family or ecclesial abuse. Some are fleeing dogmatism and triumphalism or, at least, spiritual complacency and shallowness, and a lack of hospitality to their questions and doubts. Some are yearning for a practice and language that connects rather than disconnects them from the life of the world. Others are new to the Christian tradition altogether. Some are meditators. Some are not. The common denominator is that (like those drawn to the earliest

---

30. Bonhoeffer, *Ethics*, 61–62.
31. Bonhoeffer, *Ethics*, 63.

meditation groups established by John Main)[32] those who come are seeking a deeper encounter with God, with themselves, and with others. They are in search of an authentic, mature, and evolving way of faith and doubt, a truer and more reconciled humanity. In developmental terms, most are moving from being "socialized" to "self-authoring" or "transforming" selves.

So they come to Benedictus seeking a community and practice of faith that is hospitable, truthful, unthreatened, and noncoercive, a place they can be on the way at their own pace, allowed to be who and where they are while at the same time encouraged to grow in understanding and love. All this seems profoundly important and right. It is at the heart of the ethos of contemplative church and its vocation for the world. And yet, enabling the possibility of this space of truthfulness and transformation involves certain kinds of discipline and commitment.

Practicing hospitality is not the same as "anything goes"; being nondogmatic, open to questions, and unthreatened by other traditions does not mean giving up on orthodoxy. The too glib distinction between progressive and conservative expressions of Christianity is misleading, and a contemplative church will not fit neatly into this supposed dichotomy. Maggie Ross puts it well, saying: "The person [the church] who tries to live from silence is both 'liberal' and 'conservative'; liberal, because he or she is aware from within (as opposed to bowing to a rule imposed from without) of the importance of approaching others with a wide and generous inclusiveness; conservative, because within that inclusiveness such a person wishes to conserve the fullness of what it means to be human, along with the natural world from which that humanity arose without which humanity will perish."[33]

Jesus said, "Enter through the narrow gate; for the way is wide and the road is easy that leads to destruction, and there are many who take it. For the gate is narrow and the road is hard that leads to life, and there are few who find it" (Matt 7:13–14). What in practice constitutes this narrow gate? In the rest of this chapter, I want

32. Main, *Monastery Without Walls*, 9.
33. Ross, *Silence*, 222.

to focus more directly on the foundational commitments and disciplines for the being of contemplative church. They pertain to the theology, prayer, and institutional location of such communities.

Theology

At Benedictus, we do not recite either the Apostles' or the Nicene Creed as a regular feature of our liturgy. This does not mean we are a non-creedal community. The philosopher Ludwig Wittgenstein drew an important distinction between showing and saying. There are truths or meanings we come to know only as they show themselves in practice or behavior, in forms of life and the transformation of understanding. They cannot be communicated simply by means of saying them in words, no matter how authorized.[34] Thomas Merton suggested something similar in a reflection on one of his brother monks, Father John of the Cross. Father John, said Merton, is "one of the few men in this monastery who have anything to say in a sermon. . . . What he preaches is really the Gospel, not words about the Gospel or knowledge of the Gospel, or yet knowledge of Christ. It is one thing to preach Christ, another to preach that one knows Christ. I know the integrity of this man is very costly to him."[35]

I mention these distinctions between showing and saying, between knowing and knowing about, because in my view a contemplative church is committed in the first instance not to ensuring the mere profession of orthodoxy or express conformity to doctrine, but to the awakening to living truth. We are concerned with the shift from ideas to knowledge, from conformation to transformation. Ultimately this awakening is the gift of the Spirit, but the question is, how to participate in this possibility, how to help open the way?

I know some leaders seeking to enable a more awakened and contemplative practice of Christianity who are starting

---

34. Wittgenstein, Letter to B. Russell, para. 1.
35. Merton, *Conjectures*, 159.

within existing congregations and denominational structures. Many members of these communities have imbibed their faith as part of their socialization and identify strongly with certain ways of expressing it. In such contexts, talk of the distinction between knowing and knowing about Christ, or any break with traditional or conventional forms of language and rite, may be perceived as deeply threatening. Holding established forms more lightly, allowing space and silence to be open in a different way, can feel for some like the loss of faith, like falling away rather than growth.

The challenge for a new community like Benedictus can be different. I have said that many who come to us are in a process of leaving behind former ways of practicing their faith, or have no Christian background at all. These people are likely to find some of the traditional forms and language alienating, and are looking for what they see as more "authentic" expressions. They are drawn to silence and the sense of meditation as part of a universal and nondogmatic spiritual wisdom, and tend to be allergic to any hint of Christian triumphalism or exclusivism. In this context, it is the particularity of Christian theology and proclamation that can seem problematic, and the question is how to create a hearing for any sense that (in the words of Rowan Williams) "we have a distinctive human destiny to show and share with the world."[36]

So, depending on the context, an emerging contemplative church faces different challenges. I take it for granted that we are all seeking to go beyond external and merely devotional expressions of faith. At the same time, we are not offering a generic spiritual "experience," spirituality as a commodity consumed on our terms to ease or augment our passage through life. Christian faith is committed to truth, not simply sincerity. It involves answerability for how we think and who we are. Canadian theologian Douglas John Hall comments that many people speak of "God" but the question is "which God?" "What is your image of this God . . . ? What kind of company does your God keep? What does your God ask of you—if anything?"[37] If we are to engage these questions

---

36. Williams, "Address to the Synod," para. 4.
37. Hall, *Cross in Our Context*, 76–77.

at any depth, then this means (I think) that theology matters, the witness of Scripture matters, the testimony of the saints and the hard-won wisdom of tradition matters. Yet, it is not always easy to hold these tensions.

At Benedictus, we celebrate Easter outdoors. We meet on a small island linked by a footbridge to the shore of a local lake. It is an exquisite little space, and over the triduum we move around it, beginning on the evening of Maundy Thursday standing among a grove of paperbark trees, the liturgy focusing not on the Last Supper but on the moment of betrayal in the garden of Gethsemane. On Friday morning, we meet at the foot of the cross leaning up against a large casuarina tree; and early on Sunday morning, we turn and face out towards water, the sky gradually lightening and the water birds bustling up from the lake's edge to share Communion with us. It is incredibly powerful to participate in these liturgies out in the natural world, joined by the sound of wind and birds, feeling the earth beneath our feet and seeking their meaning in the context of this larger life. There is also something challenging, even destabilizing. How does this intensely human drama framed by the thought world of first-century Judaism—telling of politics, betrayal, anguish, and death, and culminating in the strange and difficult proclamation of resurrection—how does this really affect *our* present reality, the ducks pottering quietly at the waters' edge, the life of the city going on oblivious, and the world still careering towards destruction?

I once met someone who memorably described the application of a Christian framework to her lived experience as like going to the movies in the middle of the day. As long as you are inside its world, it seems plausible enough. But as soon as you move outside the cinema, outside the chapel, it feels disconnected from the "real" world, a kind of illusion, an attempt to impose meaning on an infinitely larger and more tragic realm. Yet, theologically speaking, I wonder if it is precisely this juxtaposition, this sense of tension and even, at times, of incongruence, that constitutes the narrow gate through which we must pass if we are to be true to our calling to be a contemplative church? Williams has said: "At any point in its history, the Church needs both the confidence that it has a gospel to preach, and the ability to see that it cannot readily specify in advance how it will find words for preaching in particular new circumstances."[38]

This requires, I suggest, a two-fold openness and vulnerability, to the tradition on the one hand and to our lived experience on the other. Keeping faith with our tradition does not mean being convinced beyond the possibility of doubt, or losing our sense of the sheer strangeness of the gospel. It is more like the willingness to keep trusting there is something trustworthy here, approaching it with enough humility and patience to let ourselves be led into fuller self-yielding and so deeper conversion. Like Nathanael, one of the first disciples called in the Gospel of John, yielding to the encouragement of his friend to "come and see" (John 1:46); like Peter, daring to trust what he has glimpsed in Jesus despite his sense of ontological vertigo, saying, "Lord, to whom can we go? You have the words of eternal life" (John 6:48–49); like Mary Magdalene, turning and turning back again to what seemed like the death of all her hopes, refusing "to accept that lostness is the final human truth,"[39] we too keep allowing ourselves to be drawn. And if, almost despite ourselves, we continue to be disciples (learners), we may come to discover faith as a relationship and way of life. Maggie Ross speaks of Christianity as a process more than a belief system: "Christ as a way of knowing, Christ as a way of doing theology, of putting on the mind of Christ."[40]

This faith is not a hermetically sealed world view in competition with others, but more like accepting an invitation to entrust ourselves to a listening, a teaching, an undergoing of death and resurrection that gradually transfigures the way we see and feel, think and act. On this account, to have a gospel to preach is not having a possession to impart or impose. It means inhabiting particular possibilities for being, discovering its way of engaging the

---

38. Williams, *On Christian Theology*, 31.
39. Williams, *Resurrection*, 40.
40. Ross, *Silence*, 212.

The Being of Contemplative Church

human journey, and communicating from this way such that it becomes live, or at least able to be explored by others.

At its best and truest, the church has been seeking to communicate this way for two millennia, and there is wisdom and depth in words and forms that have served this communication in ages past. At the same time, it is not the repetition of the same words that guarantees our fidelity, but a live connection to the underlying action and truth of God. Tyson Yunkaporta has written of the way indigenous knowledge in Australia is distributed across multiple knowledge keepers so that no one person holds the whole picture. Nevertheless, each piece is connected to the pattern of the whole. "Authentic knowledge processes are easy to verify if you are familiar with that pattern—each part reflects the design of the whole system," he writes. "If the pattern is present, the knowledge is true, whether the speaker is wearing a grass skirt or a business suit or a school uniform."[41]

I want to say something analogous about preaching the gospel. Authentic, transfiguring knowledge shows itself in and through what is said and done; it is recognizable because of what happens around it—"faith, conversion, hope."[42] Authentic knowledge makes visible the eternal pattern of self-offering, life-generating love, which means it will be both consistent with the proclamation we have received and capable of showing itself in new forms. A church that is truly faithful, as distinct from a church merely clinging to an ideology, will be simultaneously able to hear the depth dimension of traditional formulas and confident to create new idioms apt for new circumstances. It will be able to risk finding innovative ways of representing what we are discovering and of deepening our sense of its meaning through language, image, gesture, music, and act.

The commitment to theological integrity, then, involves an active seeking of communication between past and present, bringing the wisdom and witness of our tradition across time and culture into conversation with contemporary understanding and

41. Yunkaporta, *Sand Talk*, 14.
42. Williams, *On Christian Theology*, 41.

need. It calls for engagement with the truth of our lives and of the lives of others, human and nonhuman. This requires us to be open to the world as it is, conscious of the fears, illusions, struggles, and hopes in the face of which we now must work out our salvation, and in relation to which the truth of the gospel must prove itself anew. We are called to show how the Christian way of imagining humanity and creation, its invitation to keep company with Jesus, are indeed transfiguring, not by dogmatic fiat but through the risk of live encounter. This has a range of implications for how we approach preaching, liturgy, gathering, and reflection in a contemplative church.

There are various capacities needed to sustain this theological integrity, including formation in tradition, study and intellectual rigor, self-awareness, and personal honesty. One capacity, neglected in some contexts but critical, is the awakening of the heart's knowing. The intelligence that is capable of discerning and communicating the gospel with authority is not the ordinary discursive intelligence of the thinking mind, but the fuller reason of the mind descended to the heart. This leads me to touch on what I take to be a second foundational discipline of contemplative church, the work of silence.

Prayer

It is presumably obvious that a contemplative church will prioritize the practice of silent prayer. At Benedictus we include a fifteen-minute period of meditation as part of our main service and offer daily meditation at various times during the week. There are retreats, quiet days, and occasional sessions introducing the practice of meditation to newcomers. How does this discipline of silent prayer connect to Jesus' exhortation to enter through the narrow gate?

In his foreword to Maggie Ross's book *Silence: A User's Guide*, Rowan Williams notes that there is a sentimentality around much contemporary vocabulary for contemplative practice. This vocabulary, he says, "can lure us into thinking that we are undertaking a set of tactics that will deliver commodities called spiritual experience or spiritual awareness." This is the spiritual materialism that John Main also warned of. Williams goes on, "The beginning of wisdom . . . is to recognize that what we are invited to in contemplative practice is ultimately the sheer presence of finite subject to, with, [and] in infinite act."[43]

And here is the connection with silence. If what we are called to is "sheer presence," this calls for "a relentless scrutiny" of the words, images, and habits of mind we deploy to create idols of God and ourselves, by means of which we imagine we can describe "infinite act" or bring it under our comprehension and control. Talking about God, thinking about our progress, imagining ourselves having certain experiences, and so on. "And this means," says Williams, that serious contemplative practice is "always . . . asking how what we say and do moves us towards silence: real silence, not a sense of vague devotional warmth."[44]

How, in practice, do we encourage this movement into "real silence," this real kenosis during the time of prayer that deepens our receptivity and purifies and expands our hearts and minds? At Benedictus, we do not insist on a particular method of meditation. Part of how we express hospitality, or what Maggie Ross calls "a wide and generous inclusiveness," is to invite people who come with an existing practice of meditation to continue in that way. Just as we are ecumenical with respect to the range of Christian traditions, so it has seemed right to be ecumenical with respect to methods of meditation. If people are new to meditation, I always teach from my own practice of Christian meditation. Otherwise, people are encouraged to continue in the way they know. When we began with this approach, I had particularly in mind the desire to ensure that practitioners of Centering Prayer could feel fully at home in the Benedictus community. Over time, we have drawn people who have learned to meditate in other ways, including using the Jesus Prayer, and through other faith traditions.

---

43. Williams, Foreword, ix.
44. Williams, Foreword, ix.

Does this openness, this unwillingness to specify a recommended method of meditation, constitute an avoidance of the narrow gate? Sometimes I wonder. Certainly, I discern the need to continue vigilant in relation to two perennial challenges. The first is the difficulty of encouraging people to trust the way of radical silence. All of us struggle to let go of spiritual materialism and fixation on spiritual "experience"; all struggle to get past our desire to "succeed" and our discouragement at perceived "failure." In a contemplative church, the challenge is to keep encouraging the profoundly counter-cultural realization that we are not meditating to achieve an outcome or gain a benefit, but simply and for no other reason than to behold God: "sheer presence of finite subject to, with, in infinite act."

The second challenge is to engage with the tendency to be satisfied with "vague devotional warmth" or what John Main (following John Cassian) called the "pernicious peace."[45] There can be a desire for cheap grace that bypasses the real dynamic of death and resurrection, and that shows up as a fuzzy self-generated sense of "union" with God and oneness with all. If the drift of certain Christian communities is towards judgment, rigidity, and a division between insiders and outsiders, the temptation of a contemplative church (as I experience it anyway) is a too glib universalism, as if we just are already one.

We must acknowledge that offering regular periods of meditation is no guarantee that those who participate are actually deepening the silence in the mind or finding their way to the threshold of the narrow gate. Yet I am not sure that any of this is solved by insistence on a single method. It is a matter of inspiring and encouraging people to be serious about the practice, teaching its pitfalls and disciplines, and then trusting that the real seeking of God and the practice itself will lead in the right time through the layers of spiritual ambition, illusion, and egoic control that must be pierced if we are truly to become simple, silent, and present. And here is where the witness and common life of the contemplative community is itself powerful and necessary.

45. Main, *Word into Silence*, 60.

Institutional Location

Finally, let me touch on the question of the institutional location of contemplative church. Maggie Ross has some startling words to say about this. She writes: "The juxtaposing of 'Christian' and 'institution' is a contradiction, not a paradox, and as the increasingly cacophonous twenty-first century progresses, the situation only gets worse."[46] For Ross, the fundamental missteps bound up with institutional Christianity are clerical control and the suppression of silence, both of which lead to an alienating theology and practice of the gospel.[47] There is a complex and mixed history here, which does not concern us now. But it does seem true that there is a tension (at the least) between the contemplative invitation to spiritual maturation and liberty, and much of what we experience as church. Williams, who has been at the heart of the Anglican church for decades, notes himself that in the absence of the transformation enabled by contemplative habits of detachment and self-forgetfulness, we "run the risk of trying to sustain faith on the basis of an un-transformed set of human habits—with the all too familiar result that the Church comes to look unhappily like so many purely human institutions, anxious, busy, competitive and controlling."[48]

It might seem as though a church like Benedictus, independent, ecumenical, not formally affiliated with an institution, is a kind of ideal world, free from the frustration of recalcitrant bishops, resistant parishioners, and all the baggage of establishment and bureaucracy. And it is true, we enjoy a kind of freedom. But, as I often joke, you leave the institution only to find yourself reinventing it; reinventing mechanisms for accountability, for discerning and forming leadership, managing conflict, paying insurance, and drawing up rosters. Because, of course, to sustain any community over time, some form is necessary. We cannot bypass the question of the kind of "jar" our treasure will be held in. Of course, those of us who start a new community may have more capacity to create

---

46. Ross, *Silence*, 212–13.
47. Ross, *Silence*, 199–201.
48. Williams, "Address to the Synod," para. 15.

our jar to be congruent with its contents, while some inherit some pretty clunky crockery. These differences have an impact. At the same time, it is no use getting fixated by them.

In a significant essay, "The Importance of Being Indifferent," theologian James Alison points out the remarkable extent to which Jesus was indifferent to the institution that dominated the religious landscape of his day, the temple system in Jerusalem. He came and went, he taught in and around it, but he did not spend his energy fighting it, trying to reform it, or asking for its approval. Alison notes that the indifference or detachment manifest in Jesus with regard to the temple was not haughty dismissal accompanied by a sense of superiority. It was more like the freedom that arises when something has ceased to push your buttons, either negatively or positively; you are neither repelled nor attracted, neither resisting it nor desperate to win it over. This freedom becomes possible, says Alison, "because your heart is pointing somewhere else, and whatever happens or doesn't happen to this thing, you will in any case have your center of gravity pulling you in quite a different direction, one which is in no way reactive, but creative of something else."[49] In this context, the narrow gate through which a contemplative church must pass is between conformity and reactivity, so to find the truly generative space of liberating obedience to the Spirit.

The church's one foundation is Jesus Christ her Lord. Our task is to seek to be faithful to what we discern of the call of Christ in the contexts in which we find ourselves. Depending where we start, we will experience different constraints and possibilities; all forms (to varying degrees) both *contain* and *constrain* the gift, and the institutional location of contemplative congregations, contemplative churches, may vary considerably. The key is not to become obsessed either with obtaining recognition, success, and validation, or with reacting to what we may perceive as the institution's failures. There will be challenges to face, obstacles to overcome. Just get on with it. If we are indeed responding to a divine call, there will be a way. As Alison puts it, "We don't need the Temple's authority to develop a shepherding. On the contrary, receiving

---

49. Alison, "Importance of Being Indifferent," 121.

The Being of Contemplative Church

Christ's heart for his sheep means receiving an authority to develop a shepherding in the midst of the collapse of the Temple. We can trust that if a ministry is from God, it will eventually be found to be in harmony with the universal *ecclesia* which is emerging as those called out of darkness together to share in God's unimaginable light."[50]

CONCLUSION

Many are drawn to the idea of contemplative church. In this chapter, my aim has been to engage with some of what I think it means to put flesh on this idea. I have focused on commitments and disciplines that to me seem foundational: commitments to theological integrity, to real silence, and to a nonreactive relationship to the institutions in and around which a contemplative church emerges. In what follows, I want to continue putting flesh on the possibility of contemplative church by articulating an approach to contemplative common worship.

---

50. Alison, "Importance of Being Indifferent," 127.

— 2 —

APPROACHING CONTEMPLATIVE WORSHIP

OF ALL THE THINGS spiritual communities do, worship is the one thing that has no parallel in other gatherings. Other groups meet to offer service and work for justice; they meet for friendship and mutual support; they may even meet to reflect about their lives and vocations, to seek transformation in themselves and their relationships. But *worship*? Directing our attention to the reality we call God, invoking and addressing God, singing and praising, listening for and yielding to God, opening our lives to that which is infinitely beyond what we can control or understand—that is something different entirely. And when our friendship and community, our service and work for justice flow out of worship—well, they are different too.

Maggie Ross speaks of worship as "beholding," the self-forgetful presence to and gazing upon God that transfigures. Worship at Benedictus (as in most Christian churches) involves a cluster of activities that serve this movement towards beholding. We gather and become present to ourselves, each other, and the world in which we meet; we participate in a liturgy, hear Scripture read and preached, share music, silence, and sacrament. Ross writes: "Good liturgy . . . leads us gently to pay attention to our struggles, our emotional state, our suffering. It then subtly attracts our attention towards a vanishing point even as these memories are flitting across the screen of the mind. Gradually, through a succession of signs presenting and effacing, good liturgy draws us into an imageless, timeless, Love."[1]

At Benedictus, we do not use a set form for our liturgy from prayer book or missal. We create the liturgy each week, drawing from resources such as the Iona Abbey worship books[2] and other contemporary sources, from poetry, the psalms, and traditional collects, as well as writing our own prayers, responses, and blessings. We draw from a range of musical styles, from traditional hymns and chants to contemporary worship songs to so-called secular music. We do not have our own church building, and we meet in a hall whose windows open into a garden we have landscaped and planted. Our aesthetic is simple and to some extent constrained by the fact that we share the space with other groups, but we seek to attend to the soul's need for beauty, using color, candles, art, and symbols from the natural world—leaves, rocks, water, and our Benedictus bonsai trees.

Once, early in the life of the community, one of our members still involved in their Catholic parish said they loved how informal the Benedictus liturgy was. A week later, one of our members coming from a progressive Uniting Church background commented on the formality of our liturgy, describing us as "high church." I thought, "You have no idea!" But I also understood what she meant. Although the liturgy is fresh each week, it follows a regular pattern, the same elements recurring in more or less the same order, in a traditional rhythm of call and response.

In fact, I was encouraged about these seemingly contrary perspectives on our liturgies, because I think they highlight something essential. As I have said elsewhere, contemplative liturgy is not primarily about a particular style or form of worship.[3] It does not have to mean continuously hushed tones, flickering candles, and Gregorian chant—Christianity for introverts. Ross writes,

1. Ross, *Writing the Icon*, 54.
2. We are profoundly grateful to the Iona community for so generously making its liturgies available for use and adaptation by other communities, and we share our offerings from Benedictus in the same spirit.
3. Bachelard, *Contemplative Christianity*, 94.

"No matter how simple or grand, contemplative or celebratory, the same rule of thumb applies." The real test of good liturgy is whether it can "implement its own effacement,"[4] whether it can point beyond itself to the reality of which it speaks and sings.

In other words, liturgy is not an end in itself, a performance to polish or experience to cultivate. The whole point of this work of the people is to help us become more fully present to ourselves and our world, to the anxieties, hopes, and pain we bring with us, and then to enable us to offer ourselves and our world to God, learning to see it all in the light of God's truth and love. Whether or not we use a set form or create liturgies for particular contexts and seasons, good liturgy (says Ross) "returns us to our ordinary tasks, and while our lives may not seem altered from day to day, over time we become obliquely aware that something has shifted slightly, that something has been justified ... in the sense that all our fragments have become subtly better aligned, integrated, infused with the ineffable welcome we call 'grace.'"[5] How in practice does good liturgy enable this process of alignment and integration? My sense is that it happens in different dimensions and that these are worth teasing out.

At one level, good liturgy has the power to enable the fuller alignment of head and heart. It leads us beyond words and self-conscious awareness to a deeper knowing, thus expanding our receptivity and shifting our felt sense of things. As Ross writes: it "makes something of truth available to us, the truth beyond our thoughts and ways that is God's, yet still ours, and that is in some measure the same truth."[6] Music is part of this shift from head to heart; image and symbolic action too. But the key is silence. And by silence I mean not a strained and embarrassed "when will this be over" kind of pause, but the receptive and restful silence of unselfconscious presence to and waiting on God. Unless all we do, sing, and say is sourced in and tends to this silence, then a worship service starts to feel as though it is filled with one item after another, like a poorly integrated primary school concert.

4. Ross, *Writing the Icon*, 61.
5. Ross, *Writing the Icon*, 54.
6. Ross, *Writing the Icon*, 54.

Approaching Contemplative Worship

I imagine many of us have experienced church services where, no sooner has the reading ceased or the sermon been preached than we pop up to sing a hymn, with the intercessions following hot on their heels. If what Ross calls the "dialogue with silence" is refused, then our words and actions become increasingly mechanical and shallow, "a noisy monologue."[7] The descent of the head to the heart is blocked and with it, our fuller knowing. All of this suggests that openness to silence must permeate the whole of our worship. It requires not just a set time of silent prayer as part of the service, but the allowing of space and time in the liturgy as a whole. And, of course, the more a culture of silence infuses the daily life and shared practice of a community, the deeper this silence goes. How does good liturgy function to align and integrate "our fragments"? In the first place, it is because it helps integrate the different parts of ourselves, head and heart, and so deepens our receptivity to the ineffable reality of grace.

At another level, the work of good liturgy is to send us out more fully connected to the life of the world. Years ago, in the week after Nelson Mandela died, one of our members commented that he had not known how much he needed to find a way of acknowledging and holding Mandela's passing until he felt that happening through the words, music, and silence of our liturgy. Or, to share a different example, in 2023 Australia held a referendum on whether to enshrine an indigenous Voice to Parliament in the constitution. It was a question put at the request of indigenous leaders, and seemed to many of us an important step in the long journey of reconciliation between First Nations and settler Australians. The referendum proposal did not pass, and one of our members commented on the profound alienation she experienced when, on the following day, the parish priest at the Catholic church she still attends made no mention at all of the referendum and its outcome in the Sunday service. She did not need him to make a political statement. But she did need him—and the liturgy—to somehow hold what had happened and its aftermath.

---

7. Ross, *Writing the Icon*, 52.

Relatedly, over the years we have realized the significance for a contemplative church of enabling liturgical connection with the natural seasons of the year. In the northern hemisphere, this connection is apparent. In Europe and North America, for example, the Easter celebration of resurrection is congruent with the emergence of new life in spring; the birth of Christ dawns symbolically as light in the dark of midwinter at Christmas. In the southern hemisphere, these seasons don't line up. We must celebrate the resurrection as the autumn leaves are falling, and light the Christmas candles with the sun blazing at high summer. Not only does this mean that the traditional theological metaphors and symbols are misaligned; it also means that our natural seasons lack liturgical acknowledgment or celebration.

For this reason, in addition to the universal calendar of the church's year, we have created a modest seasonal calendar of our own. For example, we have drawn on the resources of the contemplative tradition to create a midwinter gathering in July called "Dark Night of the Season" after St. John of the Cross, and a spring "viriditas" or "greening" service after Hildegard of Bingen. In developing these liturgies, we have found that our heightened connection with the natural seasons illuminates our participation in the tradition, and vice versa. Ross has written, "It is not the liturgy that sanctifies our lives; our lives are already sacred, and the liturgy tries to remind us of that."[8] When liturgy is attuned to the rhythms of the natural world, it functions to connect us to our embodiment in time and place in a spirit of gratitude and praise.

Finally, a third level at which good liturgy must function to align and integrate us involves the relationship of individual to community. As we share in silence, word, and sacrament, we come to recognize each other as recipients of the same divine welcome, sharers in the same transfiguring journey. This makes for the possibility of real fellowship and the sense of sharing a common life. Recall the words of Jonathan Rowson from the previous chapter

---

8. Ross, *Writing the Icon*, 53.

about our need to develop "a viable We,"[9] and how the church has a role in showing what this means.

In all this, it matters that our worship is accountable to truth. Liturgy is not just a collection of nice-sounding words and soothing sentiments. It is no use seeking through silence to be open to the depth dimension of our beings, to the mystery of God and one another, and then polluting or trivializing the space with words that are sentimental, tired, alienating, or meaningless. If the liturgy is to leave us subtly justified—integrated and realigned—then it is essential that it name the truth of things, that it is not unspeakably glib in the face of those struggling with loss, remorse, or fear. It is essential that it enable us to face the reality of our lives and our world more freely and courageously.

Preaching is part of this. Again, this will look different in different contexts, but over the years at Benedictus our preaching has sought to enable the integration of head and heart, worship and world, individual and community. We have explored particular books of the Bible and seasons of the church's year. We have engaged theological questions people find troubling or difficult, with series on atonement, the nature of divine action, and the way of peace, and (during the COVID pandemic) a series called "You Can't Ask That," during which people were invited to send in questions they thought they weren't allowed to voice in church. We have reflected on suffering and prayer, and sought to bring theological insight into conversation with contemporary questions, including the referendum on the Voice, marriage equality, and the ecological crisis.

Of course, much of this applies to good liturgy and preaching in any church. Yet again, it seems to me that without the deepening practice of silence and the hospitality of radical listening, many church communities struggle to open themselves in these ways, to do more than just go through the motions or be confirmed in what they already believe. Remember the distinction between knowing about and truly knowing Christ, between talking about transformation and being transformed? For this reason, before sharing practical resources and reflections on developing liturgy for

---

9. Rowson, *Metamodernity*, 33.

contemplative worship, I want to touch briefly on how the wider life of the church provides its necessary context.

A SCHOOL FOR THE LORD'S SERVICE

In what he described as his "little rule for beginners," St. Benedict specified how every part of a monk's life, from kitchen duty to the recitation of psalms, from clothing to decision-making, could become a vehicle for deepening conversion. My sense is that the depth and power of a community's worship is connected to this shared commitment to deepening conversion. What can this commitment to engage faithfully with the whole of life look like for non-residential, non-monastic contemplative communities?

Many churches seek to enable ongoing formation in faith and conversion of life through fellowship and study—small groups, Bible studies, seminar series, workshops, retreats, community service, and social gatherings. So it is with Benedictus. People meet to learn, to reflect on experience, and to share their lives in a range of contexts. We have discussion groups that engage with theology and Scripture, music and poetry, spiritual practices and sacred psychology, and questions of justice. There are contemplative walking and photography groups, an international Zoom home group, and groups that have met to share the journey of aging, formation in contemplative action, spirituality and creativity, gardening, and retreats. As I have said, much of this looks like the kind of small group and community life found in many churches, but let me draw out what I take to be a distinctive feature.

One of our longest standing groups is called "L'Chaim"—from the Yiddish toast "To life." L'Chaim is a small group in which participants are enabled to explore any dimension of their life—work, family, community, history, memory—using a disciplined process of reflection. People bring particular conversations or incidents they are surprised, troubled, or puzzled by; they come to explore habits of being and patterns of relating they find themselves stuck in or constrained by: "How come I always end up having *this* conversation with my mother?" "What is really happening in my relationship with my boss, my child, myself?" L'Chaim is not group therapy but a facilitated process for paying attention to the text of our lives in the light of grace. We do not advise or try to fix each other; rather we seek to create a space in which people can respond to the invitation to be reconciled in fuller ways. Each meeting, a participant prepares a written reflection in advance, focused on the incident or pattern they would like to explore. They are invited to respond to specific questions designed to deepen their engagement with their own experience. These include an invitation to connect their experience with a text from the theological or biblical tradition, or with a poem, song, or image. They then present their reflection to the group, whose members share what they notice: I notice you have used this metaphor several times to describe your relationship; I notice there is not much silence in this conversation; I notice your voice went flat when you read this section. We notice and then we begin to explore what has been shared, asking open, honest questions that may lead the person presenting to see or reflect on their experience in new ways and make deeper connections with the wisdom of tradition. Over time, insight may arise and the possibility of living with greater integrity and freedom.

Not everyone who comes to Benedictus participates in L'Chaim. Yet it seems to me a kind of paradigm for all our groups and offerings. This is because instead of having to pretend, as happens in some church contexts, that we have got it more or less together, in this group there is real and non-patronizing acceptance that the struggle and ambiguity of our lives is the theater of God's transforming work. Instead of some of us thinking we know what everyone else should be doing and believing, there is genuinely spacious listening that attends to and honors the particularity of people's journeys and seeks to help them discern their way.

Rowan Williams has said, "Responding in a life-giving way to what the Gospel requires of us means a transforming of our whole self, our feelings and thoughts and imaginings. To be converted to the faith does not mean simply acquiring a new set of beliefs, but becoming a new person, a new person in community with God and others through Jesus Christ."[10] But entrusting oneself to this process of holistic transformation in the context of a community presupposes a certain level of maturity and trustworthiness in the community itself. And this in turn relies on the growing capacity of members to be still, to listen beyond their initial reactivity, to be unthreatened by what looks unresolved and painful—all fruits of contemplative practice. If we are interested in enabling real transformation rather than simply conformation to a predetermined vision of "the good," then this is the kind of culture our churches must be capable of creating.

Contemplative worship, then, is enabled by and enables a whole way of being in the world. It is not, first and foremost, a matter of style but gathers the whole of us—all we do and are—in the presence of God. It recognizes that the depth of our prayer is internally related to the depth of our lives and our shared commitment to grow increasingly "fierce with reality."[11]

BY WHAT AUTHORITY? THE MARKS OF BENEDICTUS

By what authority, however, does Benedictus generate itself as a worshiping Christian community? We are not formally affiliated with any established church; we have not received letters of accreditation from an ecumenical council or any diocesan authority. I am ordained as an Anglican priest but was not working for the Anglican church when Benedictus first gathered. We simply declared ourselves to be an ecumenical worshiping community and began to meet, sharing news of our existence by word of mouth and personal contact.

In the beginning, the community was small—Saturday attendance was in the range of twelve to twenty people. We did not begin with any formally designated core group, though in practice a few people committed themselves early in our life together. The community grew slowly and steadily over the years, gradually

---

10. Williams, "Address to the Synod," para. 9.
11. This phrase is from Maxwell, *Measure of My Days*, 42.

Approaching Contemplative Worship

coming to require more formal organization. We explored possibilities of becoming a congregation or ministry unit within a denominational structure but our membership was already genuinely ecumenical. It did not seem right to put ourselves solely under the authority of one polity, and none of the available ecclesial structures seemed fit to hold or nurture what we were becoming. So we became an independent church incorporated as a nonprofit association. We adopted the financial and governance obligations attached to such entities, including regular financial reporting to members, an annual general meeting, and a Benedictus Council whose membership is discerned annually by the community as a whole. It is the council that has overall responsibility for the good governance of the community, including for the conduct and appointment of the director.[12]

These kinds of organizational considerations are clearly an important aspect of the question of authority, and part of generating a trustworthy space in which people may gather and grow. I am particularly concerned, however, with the issue of spiritual authority. The history of religions is littered with false prophets and charismatic manipulators of others, while earnest attempts at spiritual renewal end all too often in sectarianism, theological dead ends, and spiritual harm. When Jesus burst onto the scene in Jerusalem to teach and challenge, the religious establishment quite rightly asked him "by what authority" he was doing these things and "who gave you this authority?" (Mark 11:28). It remains a perennially important question.

Having said this, it is a question that pertains to all churches, not just to new and independent churches like Benedictus. Revelations in recent years of the shocking prevalence of sexual abuse and other forms of dysfunction in every established denomination mean we can be under no illusion that hierarchy, establishment, and supposed "apostolic succession" themselves guarantee anything. We have discovered that religious institutions are at least as likely to

---

12. This responsibility has also included developing the Benedictus Constitution as well as policies for dealing with conflict in the community, a Code of Conduct for Leaders, reportable conduct policies in relation to children, and so on.

function to protect their own interests as they are to serve God's justice and truth. In the wake of these revelations, disillusionment with the assertion of authority by established churches has driven many people from their former belonging and, sometimes, from Christian commitment itself. A response to the question "by what authority?" then, cannot simply appeal to the existence of structures and traditions, or established social license. As in Jesus' day, spiritual authority must be sourced and discerned differently.

At Benedictus, we seek to hold ourselves accountable in three main ways to what we sense is the call of God. First, we have committed to five marks of Benedictus. They are hospitality, silence, discernment, reconciliation and adventure. Just as, for example, the Benedictine vows of stability, obedience, and conversion of life help focus and orient the life of a Benedictine community, giving expression to a particular charism and way of Christian living, so our five marks orient us and give us touchstones for discerning our activities and ways of being.

The practice of hospitality involves a basic disposition of openness and unthreatenedness. Hospitality does not start from fixed notions of who is allowed or how things should be, but is disposed to welcome the other, the stranger, the new. It is characteristic of the biblical story that God's healing and fuller life come not by systematically rejecting or excluding the outsider, but by befriending and embracing difference, including what we may find difficult in ourselves and one another. Hospitality is a practice of welcome that transforms strangers, wounds, and even failure into friends. Silence is part of what enables this practice of radical hospitality. Through practicing the silence of the mind, we learn to hold more lightly our opinions, judgments, and obsessions, our habits of complaint, fantasy, and self-talk. Contemplative silence is a practice of self-dispossession, self-forgetting, which leads us to be more spacious with others and available for God. It is what makes true communion possible—so silence and hospitality go together.

Discernment, the capacity to live responsively, obediently, from deep listening, flows likewise out of silence. We cannot hear God unless we begin to detach from all the ways we grasp at reality on our own terms, noisily filling up the space with our agenda and demands. Discernment involves a willingness to suspend closure and wait in unknowing—a kind of humility. In a culture so opinionated, so often characterized by arrogant certainty and impatience with vulnerability and waiting, this practice of discernment is profoundly necessary for uncovering the wisdom our world needs.

As we deepen our capacity to listen at this level, we become increasingly participants in Christ's ministry of reconciliation. We learn to attend to the world as Jesus does, seeing things whole, with his mind. This undergirds the emergence of a genuinely prophetic voice, perceiving and disrupting the false peace that colludes in injustice, while remaining ever committed to the possibility of forgiveness, transformation, and reconnection. And the more we are drawn into this ministry of reconciliation, the more we recognize God's continuous advent in the life of the world, God's future drawing us on. We find ourselves more courageous and daring, willing to give ourselves wholeheartedly and hopefully to the adventure of the life of faith and the fulfilment of promise.[13] The five marks of Benedictus, then, are not just five nice ideas strung together, but are intrinsically connected to each other and mutually deepening. Remembering and practicing these marks is the first way we seek to keep faith with our calling to be a distinctive kind of Christian community.

Second, we pay attention to where the life is. How do you know when the Spirit of God is present and active? Things are alive. This does not mean they are without difficulty or struggle, or times of flatness and uncertainty. But, where the Spirit is, there is freedom, there is life (2 Cor 3:6, 17). When we first began to meet at the beginning of 2012, we committed to continuing until Pentecost that year and then to consider where things stood. As I have already said, our gatherings then were small; there was as yet no real sense of corporate identity or belonging, of being "a people." Yet it felt truly alive. For me, leading Benedictus seemed deeply vocational, a surprising

---

13. I have preached two reflection series on the marks of Benedictus, exploring their significance in more depth. They are available on the Benedictus Reflections page, in the years 2015 and 2020. See Benedictus Contemplative Church, "Reflections."

and unexpected expression of my calling to priestly ministry. There was life for others too. People kept being drawn, wanting to go deeper in prayer and community, growing in maturity and love. Life begets life, and in recent years Benedictus offerings have multiplied exponentially. They emerge from many different points in the community, initiated and led by community members, taking us deeper as well as wider. By what authority do we do these things? We sense the goodness of what is emerging, the fruit of our life together, and we have energy to continue.

Finally, the third way we seek to hold ourselves accountable and discern our fidelity to the truth of God is by practicing discernment in community. This is a key responsibility of the Benedictus Council, which meets regularly to reflect on what is happening and what is emerging. Discerning conversations happen in a range of other ways too, with individuals and small groups. We have not felt ourselves bound by notions of ministry programs (men's groups, youth groups, study groups) or by prepackaged strategies for church growth, as if there is a template we must conform to. In all things, we have sought simply to follow (obey) the leading of the Spirit as it shows up in the energies of particular people, as it makes alive certain possibilities or makes visible certain needs.

An important further dimension of our practice of discernment in community involves our connection to the wider church. The community to which our discernment is answerable is not just local, but is constituted by the *sensus fidelium* (the sense of the faithful) over time. Although we are not formally affiliated with any other church, we are not sectarian and seek to be in relationships of friendship and mutual support, both giving and receiving from others. The World Community for Christian Meditation (WCCM) has been the most significant ecclesial "friend" for me personally and for Benedictus, with many of our members also connected with WCCM groups and retreats. This connection has been an important source of encouragement and support, and we have contributed to the WCCM community in our turn through teaching, retreat leading, and offering support for other emerging expressions of contemplative church.

Approaching Contemplative Worship

From time to time, I and others connected with Benedictus are requested to lead retreats for clergy and laity through spiritual direction networks and at parish and diocesan levels across denominations. We have collaborated with other communities on events or projects. Conversely, we have invited guest teachers and preachers based in other communities to lead us in worship or study. In terms of our own teaching and preaching, we seek faithfully to transmit the inheritance of theologians and biblical interpreters through the ages. We are not inventing something from scratch, but seeking to participate in and extend a living tradition; our spiritual leaders are theologically educated and formally trained in ministry, reflective practice, spiritual direction, and a variety of retreat-leading modalities. This wider theological and ecclesial answerability is an essential dimension of our confidence to proclaim the gospel and reflects our commitment to contribute and be joined to the universal church.

By what authority is Benedictus constituted? By the authority of having discerned (as best we can) our own call, by remaining open to questioning, criticism, and awareness of our limits, by being grounded in prayer, worship, and theological scholarship, accountable to each other and in relationship with the wider ecclesia. Of course, things can still go wrong. According to Jeremiah's gloomy view, "The heart is deceitful above all else" (Jer 17:9), and the best can be corrupted by complacency, forgetfulness, inattention. This is the risk of all spiritual life, all spiritual community. There are no guarantees, just the commitment to follow as we discern ourselves led and to give as we discern ourselves directed.

CONCLUSION

I have been articulating some of how we approach common worship in a contemplative spirit, sharing the hinterland out of which our Benedictus liturgies emerge and the vision by which they are shaped. The next chapter offers examples from our liturgies with commentary. As well as offering resources that might be used or adapted by others, we hope to make explicit some of the choices and considerations that shape these words and the space between them. Our hope is that these reflections may be a resource for those called, as we are, to participate in the emergence of a more contemplative practice of church in their context and culture.

— 3 —

SHAPING CONTEMPLATIVE LITURGY

BENEDICTUS WEEKLY WORSHIP IS based on a simple liturgy, which includes a Scripture reading and theological reflection, music and vocal prayer, and a fifteen-minute period of silent meditation. Every third week we share in Holy Communion or Eucharist. The simplicity of the liturgy is expressed in the design of the service sheet, which participants are given as they arrive. The responses, songs, and prayers are printed on a double-sided A4 sheet of paper, which is folded in half lengthways. It matters that the layout is spacious, elegant, and consistent. The following is an image of a first page.

THE GIFT OF TONGUES
7 JUNE 2025
FEAST OF PENTECOST

WELCOME – Sarah Bachelard

OPENING RESPONSES

Move among us, God, give us life;
let your people rejoice in you.

Give us again the joy of your presence;
with your spirit of freedom release us.

Make generous our hearts and our listening;
restore us to ourselves and to each other.

ACKNOWLEDGING COUNTRY

GATHERING PRAYER

One Life of all, One God of love,
send upon us today your Holy Spirit
as on the day of Pentecost,
that our lives too may bear witness
to the gift of your renewing communion
and recreating power. **Amen**

SONG

Shaping Contemplative Liturgy

The basic shape of our liturgies is as follows:

Evening Liturgy	**Holy Communion**
Welcome	Welcome
Opening Responses	Opening Responses
Acknowledging Country	Acknowledging Country
Gathering Prayer	Gathering Prayer
Song	Song
Reading and Reflection	Reading and Reflection
Meditation	Holy Communion
Prayers of Intercession	Meditation
Song	Closing Responses
Closing Responses	Song
Blessing	Blessing

This liturgical shape is not strikingly different from that followed by many worshiping communities. What people often comment on, however, is the integrity of the Benedictus liturgies as a whole, and the way they balance the repetition and regularity needed to create a trustworthy container for encounter with a freshness that keeps us awake and alive.

WELCOME

Our main worship service begins at 6:00 p.m. on Saturday evenings, though for those joining online from other time zones it could be as early as 7:00 a.m. on Saturday morning. The original reason for this timing was simply that we do not have our own church building, and this was the time available to us. A happy byproduct has been that some of our members who wish to continue participating in more denominationally aligned congregations on Sunday mornings are able to do so. But a Saturday evening service requires particular attention to the process of gathering and the transition into worship.

People are coming towards the end of a day that, for those who work full time and have families, typically involves commitments to children's sports, housework, grocery shopping, and other necessities. In winter, people arrive when it is already dark and, for many, just getting there is an accomplishment. Those joining online likewise come out of a hinterland that may have been more or less fragmented and, for those coming for the first time, there is almost always uncertainty about what Benedictus is, who they will meet, and what they can expect. For all these reasons, if people are to be enabled to be present and open, feeling held enough to risk the possibility of live encounter, it is critical that they experience a sense of being met, of the space being ready, calm, and receptive, of entering into a grace there ahead of them.

During the process of people arriving and gathering, we seek to make space for the desire of some to greet and speak with others, while also (by way of music and silence) gradually moving the assembly towards stillness and presence before the liturgy formally begins. Music is a profoundly important element of all our worship, including this period of gathering. As already indicated, the offerings range from traditional to contemporary music, together with original compositions from some of our musicians, all of whom are members of the worshiping community. Each week, the rostered musicians offer a piece that leads into the service; the congregation receives it and is drawn by it across the threshold. There is a moment or two of silence, and then the celebrant or leader walks simply from the door, where they have been greeting those arriving, to the lectern and offers words of welcome.

Maggie Ross suggests that the "first few moments of a liturgy are usually indicative of what is to come. 'Good morning' signals something rather different from 'Blessed be God' or 'The Lord be with you.'"[1] Though she does not say so directly, her implication is that the former does far less than the latter to draw us into the mystery and truth the liturgy seeks to transmit. Being traditionally formed, I too find "Good morning" or "Good evening" jarring and too casual, but I am also aware that for those who are new

---

1. Ross, *Writing the Icon*, 59.

to church, the more formal liturgical greeting may be alien and alienating. Of course, there may be power in this very strangeness and difference from customary forms of greeting. Ready or not, all of us present are being called to become responsive to a deeper reality. At the same time, it seems to me there is a risk of some people feeling blocked in their participation from the outset. So we have sought a middle way. "Welcome to Benedictus—whether you are here in the hall or joining us online. A special welcome if you are here for the first time."

OPENING RESPONSES

The opening responses are the first responsive element in a Benedictus service. Inspired by the rhythm of the Iona Abbey liturgies, these responses launch us into the service proper and take many forms. Here is one example.

> You are here, O God,
> **Your Spirit is with us.**
>
> We need not fear,
> **Your Spirit is with us.**
>
> We are surrounded by love,
> **Your Spirit is with us.**
>
> You are in this place,
> **Your Spirit is with us.**

These responses were adapted from invocations in David Adam's, *Tides and Seasons: Modern Prayers in the Celtic Tradition*, but the differences may be instructive. Here is the original.

> The Lord is here,
> **His Spirit is with us.**
>
> We need not fear,
> **His Spirit is with us.**

We are immersed in peace,
His Spirit is with us.

We rejoice in hope,
His Spirit is with us.

We travel in faith,
His Spirit is with us.

We live in eternity,
His Spirit is with us.

The Lord is in this place,
His Spirit is with us.[2]

In adapting this invocation for the opening of a Benedictus service, partly my concern was to do with avoiding gendered language for God, which we seek to do wherever possible. Partly it was about the shift from what felt like a more declarative or disconnected stance—"The Lord is here: **His Spirit is with us**"—to the recognition of presence and the possibility of address: "You are here: **Your Spirit is with us.**" And partly it reflected a judgement about what would be sufficient for enabling the community to continue being gathered into the time and space of worship. Too many words, too many concepts, no matter how true and worthy, can risk dispersing and confusing rather than collecting and concentrating our hearts.

The key purpose of the opening responses is that they bring us to a simultaneous awareness of the divine reality that beckons us, the selves we bring along, and the world to which we belong. This invitation to simultaneous awakening can be offered in different keys. Sometimes we start with God and move towards us.

Lover of the unlovable,
toucher of the untouchable,
forgiver of the unforgiveable,
You, living Christ, meet us here.

---

2. Adam, *Tides and Seasons*, 47.

Befriended by the weak,
despised by the strong,
bone of our bone, flesh of our flesh,
You, living Christ, meet us here.

Sometimes, it is the other way around; we start with our need and call on God.

Now more than ever, living God,
we seek your face.

Now more than ever, loving Christ,
we need your truth.

Now more than ever, cleansing wind,
renew our zeal.

Sometimes the opening responses are strongly pastorally inflected.

We come weary,
seeking refreshment.

We come in sorrow,
seeking solace.

We come in helplessness,
seeking courage.

We come in denial,
seeking truth.

We come in faith,
seeking Your face.

Sometimes they are drawn from the Psalms and the charge comes from their being slightly more formal, as in these responses drawn from Ps 57.

Be merciful to me, O God, be merciful:
for I come to you for shelter.

> In the shadow of your wings
> will I take refuge:
> **until these troubles are over-past.**
>
> My heart is fixed, O God,
> my heart is fixed:
> **I will sing and make melody.**
>
> Awake my soul, awake lute and harp:
> **for I will awaken the morning.**

By contrast, these original responses, written by the Benedictus Liturgy Group, speak directly to the condition of those embarking on the season of Lent.

> Once again we resume our journey—
> **each year the same but different,**
> **each step takes us closer to ourselves.**
> In the distance lies the city,
> beacon of hope, focus of despair.
> Jerusalem beckons and repels.
> **There are many Jerusalems.**
>
> What crosses are we carrying,
> as we walk between hope and disappointment?
> How do we bear
> that rough wood across our shoulders?
> **We are about to find out.**

Some opening responses have a more occasional flavor, as for example these from the Feast of Pentecost:

> You have gifted us with your Spirit, O God,
> **like water poured out,**
> like a fire in the belly,
> **like a seed growing within.**
>
> Grow in us, O Spirit of God.
> **Turn our laments into prayers,**
> **our pain into the birth pangs of a new creation.**

Shaping Contemplative Liturgy

After the opening responses, there is silence and often a spoken encouragement to continue becoming present to ourselves, to the longing that draws us and the promise of being met. We listen together in and to the silence, and I can feel people arriving, agitation quieting, and the congregation's energy softening and opening out. Out of this silence comes the acknowledgment of country.

ACKNOWLEDGING COUNTRY

In the Australian context, it is now customary to acknowledge the country and custodianship of First Peoples or First Nations at most public gatherings and events. This acknowledgment can at times feel pro forma, "mere" words mechanically repeated. At other times, it can land as self-conscious virtue signaling. But in the context of worship, I find this acknowledgment of country profoundly significant. At Benedictus, we begin our acknowledgment by remembering the land on which we meet. I said earlier that the key purpose of the opening responses is to awaken simultaneous awareness of the reality we come to encounter, the selves we bring along, and the world to which we belong. Acknowledging country is a practice that reminds us of our radical belonging to the natural world and the obligations that come with this belonging. As we (largely settler Australians) remember this land, however, we necessarily remember those who were violently displaced and dispossessed by its conquest and colonization. We must therefore reckon with the truth of our own context and privilege, while also honoring the continuing custodianship exercised by traditional owners. Acknowledging country thus helps connect our worship to the whole of life, and profoundly grounds the gathering.

Many different forms of words may be used, but this is one part of the liturgy we tend to repeat in more or less the same form each week. Rather than this seeming like mechanical repetition, it is a kind of faithful repetition that takes us deeper into its meaning.

> We remember the land on which we meet. We acknowledge the Ngunnawal people as traditional custodians of this piece of God's good creation. We acknowledge the

way Aboriginal peoples' connection to country nurtures body, mind, and spirit and sustains the life and well-being of creatures. The elders teach that the land is not ours to own, but a gift to care for and delight in. If we listen deeply, we may hear in the life of the world the calling of the eternal Spirit.

GATHERING PRAYER

The final element of gathering in the Benedictus liturgy is what is traditionally called the "collect" or "gathering prayer." This prayer continues to signal the overall theme of the service and deepens the invitation to open ourselves to being touched, challenged, and changed.

One Lent, our weekly reflections were centered around the Gospel of the day in conversation with a series of paintings by First Nations artist and elder Miriam Rose Ungunmerr. The paintings, known as the *Australian Stations of the Cross*, were commissioned for the Roman Catholic Church at Daly River in the Northern Territory. They are an astonishing interpretation of the passion narrative in the light of indigenous symbols. At station two, Jesus accepts his cross, whose weight is depicted by markings on the cross itself and on Jesus' body. In her commentary, Ungunmerr wrote, "The patterns on Jesus' body show the pain the weight of the cross is causing him. He is thinking of all of us, and he accepts the cross with a great and generous heart."[3] The gathering prayer for that service drew us into contemplation of this image and its meaning for our own Lenten journey.

> Loving and present God,
> you who know us,
> may the patterns of our pain
> become the yes on our path
> that we might bear your presence. **Amen.**

---

3. Ungunmerr, *Australian Stations*, 7.

Shaping Contemplative Liturgy

The following gathering prayer for Harvest Festival invites thankfulness and holistic awareness of the rhythm of the seasons, and the texture of our days.

> Center of all,
> we are humbled by your provision
> in painful and plentiful seasons.
> Help us to weave
> this knowing into our daily living,
> O God of life's web. **Amen.**

This simple gathering prayer was offered during the season of Easter, when the reading for the day came from the Revelation to St. John:

> Living One,
> who was, and is, and is to come,
> we come before you
> in our hope and in our need.
> Be known to us
> as we are known to you. **Amen.**

During the celebration of Easter, as well as holding services on Thursday, Friday, and Sunday, we have been committed to the liturgical marking of Holy Saturday. Essayist and philosopher George Steiner famously suggested that much of human life is, metaphorically speaking, lived on Saturday, in the aftermath of the suffering and waste of Friday, and with the promise of Sunday not yet realized. In the New Testament, this in-between Saturday time is the time of the church, eschatological time, the time before the end, although in the Gospels the day is passed over in silence. "There is one particular day in Western history about which neither historical record nor myth nor Scripture make report," wrote Steiner. "It is a Saturday. And it has become the longest of days."[4]

If this is so, then the question of how to live on Saturday—remaining true to the experience of Friday and open to the possibility of Sunday—is an urgent matter, and one strangely neglected in the Easter liturgies. Indeed, the customary liturgical neglect

---

4. Steiner, *Real Presences*, 231–32.

of this discomforting, liminal day seems part of a wider, cultural resistance to bearing with what is unresolved, or to abiding in the face of what is beyond our control. In the Australian context, and perhaps this is connected with the needs of aging congregations, the Easter Vigil is often brought forward from midnight on Sunday to earlier and earlier on Saturday night; the proclamation of resurrection rings out little more than a day after Jesus' death on Friday. While this may be practically convenient, it seems a kind of liturgical formation in impatience. Rather than learning to wait on the action of God and the arising of something genuinely new, we just want a time of suffering to be over and to take its resolution into our own hands; rather than a counter-cultural trust in the power of faithful endurance that produces authentic hope (Rom 5:4), the church often seems to participate in the same anxious grasping that characterizes much of our culture.

As part of our commitment to a more contemplative way of being, then, we gather for a Liturgy of Waiting on Holy Saturday. The gathering prayer for this service names the pain of it.

> Hidden God,
> we gather tonight at the tomb
> sealed shut by a great stone,
> the light of the world gone out.
> Hope is quenched, faith a dream;
> love is pain and we do not even
> know what to pray.
> Help us, Lord; hear us, save us. **Amen.**

There is something very powerful about our Easter practice of gathering on Friday and leaving unresolved, gathering again on Saturday, and again leaving unresolved. Over the years, more and more members of the Benedictus community have committed to sharing this entire paschal journey. Part of what this means, however, is that we travel so deeply into the death of hope, connecting it with the death of hope in our own and the world's experience, that it feels impossible suddenly to spring into the triumphalist tone of many traditional Easter Sunday liturgies the next morning. We are not there yet—we are more like the women at the tomb, unsure what to think, unable simply to snap out of our experience of the days before, and unwilling to dishonor the reality of abiding and unhealed suffering in our world.[5] How then is it possible liturgically to begin to open the space for resurrection without being false and falsifying? This gathering prayer for Easter morning seeks to name the state in which we come:

> O God, so strange and unexpected,
> for days we have been mourning your end,
> and now there is news of beginning.
> Startled, confused, unsure of your meaning,
> give us patience and freedom to receive your presence.
> **Amen.**

There are also occasions on which we hold more lightly the traditional form of the collect to offer an even simpler gathering prayer. These are times when, perhaps, the troubles of the world or the mystery of God have brought us close to silence and a deep sense of our poverty and need. On the Feast of Trinity, in a context of war and terror, we prayed to be collected like this:

> Gather us in your presence, Living One.
> Awaken us to your presence within us.
> Reveal through us your presence among us. **Amen.**

Gathered, then, to ourselves, to God, and to our wider context, we sing.

SONG

In an evening liturgy, we generally sing as a congregation three times. A song comes after the gathering prayer, a chant is sung as a response during the intercessions, and the final song comes just before or after the closing responses. The choice of songs relates to the theme of the service, the availability of musicians, and the repertoire of theologically appropriate (or bearable) lyrics. Given the general ethos of Benedictus services, including the fact that

---

5. Cf. Williams, *On Christian Theology*, 39.

we meet in a hall rather than a church and do not have an organ, I tend to choose more contemporary songs than traditional hymns, though we do enjoy belting out a few old favorites. There are the usual dilemmas to do with balancing sing-ability and familiarity with freshness and surprise, as well as the struggle to source new congregational music in any systematic way. At the same time, one of the joys of our life together is the growing creativity of our musicians. The chants we sing as part of our intercessions are increasingly generated from within the community, and there are often original pieces offered before and after our worship.

Naturally, members of the congregation have different musical preferences, but it seems to me that a strength of our eclecticism is that it encourages a spirit of hospitality. Our musical range means that there is no settled ownership of style and approach; we are invited to listen beyond our natural (or conditioned) inclinations for the gifts offered week by week. It contributes to our formation in generosity and our valuing of diversity.

But why sing at all? In a recent reflection, Father Adam Bucko, director of the Center for Spiritual Imagination at the Episcopal Cathedral of the Incarnation in New York, offered a helpful insight. He wrote, "Too often, contemplative spirituality is reduced to silence and stillness. As Barbara Holmes reminds us, drawing from her own experience in the Black church, the path to Divine Presence—especially in communities shaped by suffering and struggle—often moves through sound, rhythm, and praise."[6] Referring to his own experience growing up under a totalitarian regime in Eastern Europe, he said, "It wasn't silence that saved us. It was the power of communal gatherings, where the preacher offered prophetic words that cracked open the heaviness of our lives and made space for hope. It was in the singing and in the Eucharist that we felt ourselves lifted beyond fear."[7]

For Bucko, then, contemplation includes stillness, "but it also includes the drumbeat, the dance, the lament. What matters is not the form, but the posture: a heart open to be touched, a life ready to

---

6. Bucko, "Sacred Activism," par. 2.
7. Bucko, "Sacred Activism," par. 3.

be remade."[8] Without song, the effect of a service of quiet can be to turn us more and more inward. We can end enclosed in ourselves, the energy to connect dwindling away. We sing at Benedictus, then, because music, rhythm, chanting, corporate songs of praise, invocation and lament, open our hearts in a different way, "soften our defenses, and warm our willingness to love."[9] It brings us joy.

READING AND REFLECTION

After the first song comes the reading, which is offered by a member of the congregation. As we are a "hybrid" community, with some gathering physically in the hall and others joining online, there are times when the reading comes to us from someone in another part of Australia or even another country. This generates a wondrous sense of connection and mutual presence across vast distances. It is moving, and a kind of miracle, to be in Australia and have (say) the Christmas reading brought by a member of the community who is in the UK or South Africa.

As for what is read each week, this involves careful thought. The typical pattern for communities that follow the Revised Common Lectionary is to have four readings as part of the main worship service. The idea is to ensure that over the course of a three-year cycle a weekly worshiping congregation will hear most of the Gospels and significant chunks of the Hebrew Scriptures and New Testament writings. The rule of the lectionary protects congregations from being at the mercy of the leader's scriptural preferences and idiosyncrasies, ensures that the gospel is heard in the context of its Jewish inheritance, and makes room for the varied voices and forms in which the word of God is communicated in the text of Scripture. With all these intentions, I agree.

---

8. Bucko, "Sacred Activism," par. 5

9. Bucko, "Sacred Activism," par. 11. Bucko refers here to the work of Andrew Harvey, who identifies five paths for expanding receptivity and cultivating courage to consent to God acting through us. Song and dance are included in the "warm practices," whereas silent meditation is one of the "cool practices."

And yet, at Benedictus, we almost always have only one reading from Scripture. Partly this is to do with time. We are committed to the fifteen-minute period of meditation in every service. We want pauses and silence to permeate the whole liturgy, and for the service to run in total not much longer than an hour. Four readings take too long. But this practical consideration is not the most significant reason for our choice. The deeper reason is to do with the possibility of real and transformative engagement with the text.

I have said I value the lectionary's intention to enable the fullest possible encounter with Scripture. In practice, however, four solid readings often function in precisely the opposite way, occurring as a largely impenetrable wall of words with not enough space for digestion. Add these to the deluge of words most people are subjected to, day in and day out, from news, social media, and the demands of workplaces and bureaucracy, and the effect is numbing. Our priority, therefore, is not to download as much biblical content as possible, but to create and guard space for deeper listening. Moreover, for many contemporary congregations, the thought world of the biblical text is profoundly foreign, if not actively alienating. Even those with deep roots in the Christian tradition may have limited capacity to contextualize what they are hearing, or may not have the theological wherewithal to listen beyond the literal. The preacher is charged with enabling access to the living word, but in practice cannot usually engage the nuances and complexity of every reading. The focus of the homily or reflection is necessarily on one text or theme, which may leave a bunch of unsatisfactory loose ends in the congregation's mind, or simply a sense of disconnection between all the elements. In which case, what really has been achieved by including them all?

Yet if you choose only one text, on what basis do you do so? At Benedictus, we keep in tune with the lectionary in the sense that we follow the liturgical calendar and the three-year cycle of the Gospels—the years of Matthew, Mark, and Luke, with bits of John interspersed. The bulk of our preaching is from the Gospel reading set for the day, though at least one whole series of reflections each year focuses on a book from the Hebrew Scriptures. Over the years, we have reflected on the books of Exodus, Genesis, the Elijah cycle, Ruth, Job, and a range of prophetic books. Similarly, in seeking to honor the breadth of the New Testament writings, we have had series focusing on the Acts of the Apostles, on letters of Paul and Peter, and on the book of Revelation.

In all this, the notion of "series" is key to our approach to preaching. Although there are weeks where the theme and reflection stand alone, a regular feature of our worshiping life is to embark on a series of connected reflections over a three, four, or six-week period. As a preacher, I find it satisfying and stretching to have the time and space to delve more deeply into a biblical book or theological theme and, for the congregation, this allows for the possibility of deepening understanding and engagement with the word. We make the reflections available on our website, and people say they reread them, wonder about them, catch up with ones they have missed. There are obviously times in the liturgical calendar that lend themselves to this approach—the seasons of Lent and Advent, for example, and the season of Creation. We also generate these mini-seasons for ourselves in Ordinary Time as a way of offering a sense of focus and intention.

As well as allowing for the exploration of texts or themes in depth, a reflection series may emerge in response to other promptings. For example, we have had several "Call and Response" series, where members of the congregation share something of their own spiritual journey—their journey of "call and response"—and prepare their reflection in conversation with a biblical passage that has been significant to them. We have also had series in response to particular circumstances. During the COVID lockdown in Australia, we offered a series of reflections based on the Psalms called "How Long, O Lord?" which explored the experience of prolonged suffering and the practice of lament. Another was called "God of Small Things," reflecting on God's action in those who lived what might have seemed small or hidden lives, Charles de Foucauld and Thérèse of Lisieux. Then, emerging from COVID, we reflected on the theme of "Interiority and Recovery," bringing emerging public policy discussions on the shape of "recovery" into conversation with Scripture and a theological perspective. Although I have said that mostly we have only one reading, there are occasions when we bring a second text into dialogue with the Scripture of the day. "*Poetica Divina*" is a recurring series that involves reading a poem alongside a biblical text and reflecting on what emerges from their juxtaposition.[10] There are also occasions where we have reflected on Scripture in relationship to visual art—Miriam Rose Ungunmerr's *Australian Stations of the Cross*, images of Jesus' baptism, images of the Last Supper, and so on.

In a whole range of ways, then, we are seeking to bring the wisdom of God to bear on the realities of our lives and the truth of our time. This is also why we speak of "reflections" rather than "sermons" or "homilies." We are seeking to share not a finished interpretation of a text or theme but an invitation to those present to reflect on their own experience and understanding in the light of the witness of tradition and the practice of prayer, to provoke a dialogue that may deepen over time.

HOLY COMMUNION

In our non-Eucharistic evening liturgies, after the reading and reflection, we move directly into silent meditation. I will say more about this transition shortly. Every third week, however, we move from the reflection into Holy Communion. Why every three weeks?

Again, a range of considerations are in play. When Benedictus first began as an ecumenical worshiping community, I was conscious that the question of sharing the Eucharist could be difficult for some. Not all churches encourage participation beyond denominational boundaries, particularly when the celebrant is a woman. I did not wish some who might otherwise be drawn to participate in our contemplative church to feel excluded by a weekly Eucharistic celebration.

---

10. Twelve of these reflections, delivered over a three-year period, have been published in Bachelard, *Poetica Divina*.

Shaping Contemplative Liturgy

At the same time, nor did it feel right for us to be a non-Eucharistic community. Sharing this sacrament is integral to the practice of Christian faith, and there are many for whom Benedictus is their only church—they have no other parish or congregational belonging. It mattered, therefore, that we celebrate Communion together. In the end, a rhythm of Eucharist every third week seemed right. A month seemed too long, fortnightly a little too regular; every third week generated a sense of the specialness and anticipation of these services, while also honoring our sense that the silence of meditation at every service is itself a sacrament of real presence.

In traditional liturgies, the movement into the Eucharist begins with a prayer of approach. These prayers usually take the form of a declaration of our unworthiness or confession of sin, which leads then to the proclamation of absolution and the assurance of divine welcome. I believe it is indeed necessary to approach the Eucharist "poor in spirit" and conscious of our need of grace. I am uneasy with the resistance to any call to humility or repentance displayed by some expressions of contemporary spirituality. At the same time, traditional prayers of humble access or corporate confession can often do more harm than good. Rather than evoking a true and healing awareness of our need, blindness, and hurt, their effect (at least for those who have suffered abusive religious histories) can be either unhealthily denigrating or provocative of resentment. They can thus close rather than open people to the goodness and mercy of God.

For this reason, at Benedictus we tend to offer what we call a "prayer for mercy" rather than a corporate confession as the preface to the greeting of peace. We are drawn more fully into the state of receptivity by bringing to our awareness, not just our personal "sins" and failings, but also our wounds and longings. The following prayer for mercy was part of a service where the reading from Rom 5:1–5 spoke of our sufferings producing endurance and endurance producing hope, and of hope not disappointing us.

> Living God, in our fear and distress,
> we struggle to keep open space for you.
> Help us to endure our suffering in hope,

that we may come to bear your presence in our world.
Amen.

This prayer for mercy offered during the season of Lent was based on Ps 25:

> To you, O Lord, we lift up our hearts.
> In you we place our trust.
> **Show us your ways, teach us your paths.**
> **Guide us in your truth.**
>
> Turn to us and be gracious to us,
> for we are lonely and afflicted.
> **The troubles of our hearts have multiplied**
> **in this season of suffering.**
>
> May our integrity protect us,
> as we take refuge in you.
> **Free us from our anguish.**
> **All our hope is in you.**

There are occasions where it does seem right to offer a prayer of confession, as in this longer prayer on the Feast of All Souls.

> God of the living, God of the dead,
> your mercy is sure,
> your will is always to reconcile and free.
>
> We remember in your love
> those who have gone before us—
> those we loved and who loved us,
> those who caused us pain
> and with whom we were at odds,
> those who died alone,
> and all victims of violence and hate.
> *(Silence is kept.)*
> **May your grace light their way.**
>
> We hold before your reconciling gaze,
> all in our own lives that separates us
> from each other and from you—
> the grief that disintegrates and makes us bitter;

the injustices suffered we have not forgiven;
the things we have done or left undone that cause suffering for others;
the wrongs in which we are complicit whether we know it or not, will it or not.
(*Silence is kept.*)

God of the living, God of the dead,
you know our hearts.
We turn to you,
we turn from fear and evil.
Give us grace to enter your love,
and choose your way of life.

In a traditional Anglican liturgy, the greeting of peace follows from the absolution. Here an extended introduction to the greeting of peace serves as a prayer of approach. This was offered when the reading was from Song of Songs, during the season of Pentecost.

When we believe
we have never tasted your love;
when we lack
the contentment of your peace;
when we feel unmet
in the deepest places of the heart;
when we are unaware
of being cherished by you;
may we know you are ever with us,
desiring that we awaken to your presence.

May the peace of Christ be with you.
And also with you.

We then share the greeting of peace and move into the prayer of consecration itself.

Many traditional prayers of consecration can be hugely wordy, whole Eucharistic theologies expressed as prayer. There can be something important in these attempts to distill the meaning of the sacramental act; there can also be something distracting and distancing. At times these prayers feel like battles from the Reformation reenacted in the hearing of those who know little of the disputes in question and care less. Yet to depart from some of these traditions can also feel risky and potentially ungrounding; some contemporary Eucharistic liturgies are just as wordy and inclined to sentimentality. Our approach, therefore, has been to heed the essential lineaments of ancient traditions, while also seeking to simplify and make fresh the act of consecration.

We tend to use two main forms for this prayer. The first retains the shape and responses of the mass—the sursum corda ("lift your hearts"), the Sanctus ("holy, holy, holy"), the memorial acclamation ("Christ has died, Christ is risen, Christ will come again")—and concludes (Anglican style) with the Lord's Prayer. As in many liturgies, traditional and contemporary, the preface varies according to the season or theme. There are also occasions when we vary the text of the responses to avoid the language of "lordship," which can function to misidentify the character of divine power.[11] For example, in place of the traditional

> Lift up your hearts.
> **We lift them up to the Lord.**
>
> Let us give thanks to the Lord our God.
> **It is right to give our thanks and praise.**

we offer this:

> We lift up our hearts,
> **that we may praise God.**
>
> Let us give thanks to the God of grace.
> **It is right to give our thanks and praise.**[12]

---

[11]. I understand the confession of Christ as "Lord" is supposed to subvert the assumption that power is about domination (people "lording it over" one another). However, the sense of subversion is generally lost in contemporary hearing, which means the meaning received is not the meaning intended.

[12]. See full text for this prayer of consecration in chapter 5.

A second form we use for the prayer of consecration is drawn largely from the Iona liturgies. Though still led by a celebrant, this form involves more of a sense of concelebration, involving the people and priest together.[13] After the prayer of consecration, we recite the Lord's Prayer. Often it is the lightly modernized version found in *A Prayer Book for Australia*,[14] but we have also developed a version of this prayer that seeks to be mindful of contemporary sensibilities to do with gender and the language of sin.

> Loving source of our life,
> God of us all,
> reverenced may you be,
> may your justice come,
> your will for the world be realized.
> Give us this day our daily bread.
> And free us from that which binds us,
> as we become those who unbind others.
> Do not let our suffering overcome us,
> and save us from the power of destruction.
> For you are ever present and your love is true,
> now and forever. **Amen.**

It seems to me that both these versions of the Lord's Prayer are important. It is not just that the familiar version appeals to traditionalists and the more contemporary version to others. One of our members has had very little connection with church, and I had assumed the more contemporary paraphrase would speak to her best. In fact, she once told me, it is the traditional form that is most meaningful. It connects her back to very early childhood and a grandmother who prayed with her. Conversely, there are others for whom the paraphrase opens out the essential dynamics of the prayer Jesus taught, without the blocks that, for them, are embedded in the older words. In all this, the motivation for alternating and adapting is not a vain attempt to please all the people all the time, but to inhabit our words in ways that lead to life.

---

13. Iona Community, *Iona Abbey Worship Book*, 149–50.
14. Anglican Church of Australia, *Prayer Book for Australia*, 141.

MEDITATION

After we celebrate Communion, we move directly into meditation. When there is no Communion, the meditation follows the reflection. Whereas during our daily online meditation sessions, we meditate for twenty or twenty-five minutes, during the Saturday service the meditation is fifteen minutes. Why only fifteen?

Incorporating a serious time of meditation into the service is a nonnegotiable part of our liturgy. We want to be a community that practices praying contemplatively together rather than just talking about contemplation and recommending it. At the same time, in the context of an hour-long service and the attendance of those who are new to meditation, a fifteen-minute session is more manageable (and, for some, quite challenging enough). As discussed in the first chapter, during this period we encourage those with an existing practice of silent meditation to continue in the way they know. This is an expression of hospitality to practitioners of approaches such as Centering Prayer and the Jesus prayer, as well as practitioners of breath or body-based methods. For those new to meditation, we suggest the method taught by the World Community for Christian Meditation.

There is a natural flow from the reception of Holy Communion into this time of silent meditation, but some comment that they find it a difficult transition when the meditation comes directly after the reflection. Although we deliberately leave quite a lengthy pause between these elements, some still struggle to move from word to silence, from thinking to simple receptivity. I have wondered about relocating the time of meditation to earlier in the service, but in the end two considerations have seemed decisive.

One is to do with the significance of how any silence is framed. As Rowan Williams has noted, silence is never neutral. "We cannot imagine an 'unframed' or pure silence. . . . Silence for us is always the gap that occurs *here*, in this specific place between words or images."[15] There is all the difference in the world, for example, between the charged and stressful silence that descends on

---

15. Williams, *Edge of Words*, 157; emphasis original.

Shaping Contemplative Liturgy

a household after an argument, and the peaceful, companionable silence of contented togetherness. "To talk about silence," Williams goes on, "is always to talk about *what specifically* we are not hearing; or what we decide not to listen to in order to hear differently; or what specifically we find we cannot say."[16] In a Benedictus service, our time of silent meditation is framed by having heard and reflected on the word and act of God. We have spoken of the loving and merciful reality before whom we are now invited to present ourselves without defense and without remainder. And it is this framing, the reading and reflection together with all that has preceded these—the welcome, gathering, and song—that is part of enabling the trust required for offering ourselves ever more wholly in the silence of pure prayer.

Second, it seems to me that our shared silence in the wake of the reading and reflection functions as a kind of accountability to the truth we never master or exhaust. When I trained for ministry, one of my teachers suggested that a reason for saying the Nicene Creed after the sermon in a traditional liturgy is that, whatever has been said on a particular occasion by a particular person, however faithfully or not the word has been shared and heard, the Creed restates the heart of faith. "We believe in one God . . . ; we believe in one Lord, Jesus Christ, the only Son of God."[17] At a Benedictus service, the shared silence functions in an analogous way. But rather than reciting the Creed aloud together, declaring the mystery of our shared faith in words, we simply allow ourselves to be receptive to it, seeking to "hear differently." All our words and attempts to understand, necessary as they are, are also revealed to be penultimate. Meditation at this point in the service is an invitation to yield to another wisdom.

After meditation, in a service of Holy Communion, we move directly into the closing responses. In an evening liturgy, we turn after meditation to the prayers of intercession.

---

16. Williams, *Edge of Words*, 157; emphasis original.
17. Anglican Church of Australia, *Prayer Book for Australia*, 123.

PRAYERS OF INTERCESSION

For many of those drawn to Benedictus, intercessory or petitionary prayer presents significant theological difficulty. They struggle with the whole notion of divine intervention and what it means to petition God for particular outcomes, as well as with how to address God and position ourselves in relation to God. This may be why they are drawn to the practice of silent, contemplative prayer in the first place. I resonate with many of these difficulties, and yet my own experience is that, over time, the prayer of the heart leads us back to words and the desire to intercede for the life of the world.

By "intercede," I do not mean trying to attract the attention of a God who is otherwise neglectful or indifferent to our suffering, nor putting in an order for our personally approved state of affairs. It is more about the desire of our transfigured hearts to join *with* God, who, in Christ, intercedes for us. In the Christian vision, Jesus comes to mediate God's love for us. His intercession makes bridgeable the gap between the life for which we are made and all that separates and alienates us from God and one another. If this is so, then the more we are drawn to him, through silence and deep listening, the more our prayer and our life joins to his. We find ourselves desiring to offer our attention, our love, our heartache, our action, and our words in service of his ministry of reconciliation, his divine yearning for the good of all.

In many Christian contexts, these public prayers of intercession are handed over to members of the congregation. In some traditions, people may be invited to offer spontaneous, spoken prayer; in others, a rostered individual prepares the prayers and leads them on behalf of all. There is an important theological truth expressed by this participatory leadership. In some contexts, it is the only point of "newness" in the liturgy, and such prayers can function to bind the community strongly together, as well as connecting a community to its care and responsibility for the world. Those with the gift of intercession minister deeply to the whole.

At the same time, this free-form participatory approach can also be fraught. From prayer leaders who smuggle in homilies under the guise of intercession to those operating from naïve theologies of episodic divine action, there are ways of praying for others and ourselves that can be profoundly unhelpful. For this reason, at Benedictus we integrate the spoken prayers as part of the liturgy. These prayers reflect the vulnerability and truth into which the silence has led us and seek to be pastoral as well as prophetic. Their content is necessarily occasional, and although there are variations in form, they are usually offered with a responsive chant. We avoid gendered language, and I am wary of too many uses of phrases such as "we pray" or "we ask." More often than not, our prayer is an expression of holding, bringing, or remembering before God the concerns of our hearts and the travail of the world, entrusting our longings and needs to grace.

Here is one example from the season of Easter, where the reflection was based on the story of Jacob's ladder in Gen 28 and Thomas Merton's famous words about the light of God shining in everyone.[18] The prayers incorporate a chant written by one of our musicians.

> *Shine, Lord, shine. Shine, Lord, shine.*
> *In the cracks across this crazy world, in the caverns of my mind.*
> *Shine, Lord, shine. Shine, Lord, shine.*
> *Through fissures in our fractured lives,*
> *Shine, Lord, shine.*[19]

> The gate of heaven is everywhere, the glory of the Lord is all around,
> yet our vision is obscured.
> Obscured by self-preoccupation and inattention,
> by anxiety, fearfulness and trauma, by prejudice and busy-ness.

---

18. Merton wrote, "It is like a pure diamond, blazing with the invisible light of heaven. It is in everybody, and if we could see it we would see these billions of points of light coming together in the face and blaze of a sun that would make all the darkness of cruelty of life vanish completely.... I have no program for this seeing. It is only given. But the gate of heaven is everywhere." Merton, *Conjectures*, 158.

19. Words and music by Neil Millar. Used by permission.

Help us to see the secret beauty in those around us,
even when they annoy and disappoint us,
when they mirror that which we reject and dislike in ourselves. *(Silence is kept.)*
Living Light, help us to see. *(Chant)*

The gate of heaven is everywhere, the glory of the Lord is all around,
yet the earth is in thrall to brutality and terror.
We remember those who are hungry and despairing, imprisoned and abused;
we cry out with the people of Gaza and the occupied territories,
and with the people of Sudan, Ukraine, and the Congo,
against the hard-heartedness of arms dealers and corrupt regimes. *(Silence is kept.)*
Living Light, transfigure our life together. *(Chant)*

The gate of heaven is everywhere, the glory of the Lord is all around.
You are in this place. In silence, we yield ourselves anew . . .
Living Light, make us bearers of your life. *(Chant)*

The intercessions begin, then, to gather the threads of the whole service—the selves we have brought with us and our care for the world, the dialogue with Scripture and silence, and the reality that God's goodness and promise can at times feel painfully absent from our lived experience. The intercessions should leave us with a sense that the truth has been named, the tensions held in the face of mystery, and access to grace left open. All this is finally expressed or held in the closing responses.

CLOSING RESPONSES

The closing responses continue our transition from the work of the liturgy to our life in the world. They prepare us to return to our tasks, responsibilities, and households with (as Maggie Ross puts it) "all our fragments . . . subtly better aligned."[20] In some way, they sum up or encapsulate the gifts we have been given and send us out with the encouragement to go on, more faithful, hopeful, truthful, free. Often our closing responses are in the same form as the opening responses, once again inspired by the practice of the Iona Abbey. These, for example, were written for the season of Advent.

> May we keep heart
> through the pain of our remaking.
>
> **May we keep faith**
> **through the long days of our waiting.**
>
> May we find you
> in hidden places and unguarded moments.
>
> **May we recognize you**
> **in the miracles of dailiness.**

These responses were from a service whose theme was the Sabbath day.

> Living Christ, you see through
> the masks that block real love.
> **Masks of piety, masks of anxiety,**
> **masks of activity, masks of denial.**
>
> Where complacency keeps us separate,
> where overwhelm makes us apathetic,
> where complexity turns us simplistic,
> **let us be emptied of untruth,**
> **and sourced in your giving life,**
> **so to bear your compassion and rest.**

Although most closing responses aim to name what we have shared in the key of resolution or at least hope, there are occasions where it seems right to leave things more unresolved. These are from early in the season of Lent.

---

20. Ross, *Writing the Icon*, 34.

In this Lent
hear our laments:

**for the limits of our humanity
and our powerlessness to save those we love,**

for our failure
to give what is needed

**and our broken dreams
for a just and peaceful world.**

Likewise, these closing responses from the Holy Saturday liturgy are particularly challenging, since there is no blessing at the end of this service. We leave things here and depart in silence.

God in the tomb,
the silence,
the darkness,
the place of the dead,
we wait...

God of the aching in-between,
we wait...

God of the long day's journey of Saturday,
we wait...

Sometimes, rather than inviting congregational responses, we close with a prayer or poem. Poems come from a range of sources, including those written by members of the congregation, as well as from writers as varied as Australian poets Michael Leunig, James McAuley, and Judith Wright; English poet-priests George Herbert and R. S. Thomas; contemporary voices such as Czeslaw Milosz, Padraig O'Tuama, Marie Howe, Mary Oliver, and Nicola Slee; Sufi poets Hafiz and Rumi; and the more directly liturgically oriented poetry of Jan Richardson, Malcolm Guite, and Meister Eckhart.[21] As well as giving the joy of fresh ways of seeing and knowing our

---

21. For Eckhart, I recommend Jon Sweeney and Mark Burrows, *Meister Eckhart's Book of the Heart*.

world, the use of poetry towards the end of a liturgy offers a resource to take with us into the week and a real connection to the communion of saints.

BLESSING

After the final congregational song, our spoken liturgy concludes with a blessing. These are performative speech acts. They effect what they say, continuing to strengthen the good in us and empowering us to participate in God's goodness and love for the world. Often we use traditional forms of blessing. These include the Aaronic blessing ("May the Lord bless you and keep you..."[22]), the Grace ("The grace of the Lord Jesus Christ, the love of God, and the communion of the Holy Spirit..."[23]), and the beautiful words of St. Paul ("The peace of God which passes all understanding...").[24]

In keeping with our general practice of minimizing gendered language for God, we tend to name the Trinitarian life in "economic" terms—"Creator, Redeemer, and Giver of Life" or, more usually, in the words of the New Zealand Prayer Book, "Earth-maker, Pain-bearer, Life-giver."[25] Variations on this Trinitarian naming include this, from the Feast of the Trinity:

> Most blessed Trinity,
> may we so share in your divine life,
> that our lives bear your reconciling love for the world.
> And the blessing of the Three-in-One,
> God for us, God with us, God in us,
> be among us, now and forever. **Amen.**

This blessing was from Advent when the reading was of the Annunciation.

---

22. Num 6:24–26.
23. 2 Cor 13:14.
24. Anglican Church of Australia, *Prayer Book for Australia*, 144.
25. Church of the Province of New Zealand, *New Zealand Prayer Book*, 181. This text is itself adapted from Cotter, *Prayer at Night*, 42.

> And now may the blessing of God,
> Begetter, Begotten, and Midwife of love,
> be with us and remain with us. **Amen.**

This was from Set Pools of Silence, our service at the height of summer.

> Go now in the service of God's world.
> Listen to the cry of the earth and of stifled souls,
> and become for them a source of refreshment—
> a channel for living water, a pool of compassionate silence, a hospitality for joy.
>
> And may the blessing of the God of life,
> the Christ of love, and the Spirit of grace,
> be upon you this day and evermore. **Amen.**

At other times, the Trinitarian emphasis is more muted or implicit. This blessing from the Feast of All Saints plays on the name "Benedictus" (meaning blessed), and the sense of our vocation as a community.

> May the Spirit who enfolds the saints
> enable us to unfold our hearts, and
> discover the truth of our lives.
> And as we yield ourselves like them,
> may we too be transfigured by the light of eternity,
> blessed to be a blessing. **Amen.**

After the blessing, the leader of the service walks from the lectern at the front of the hall back to the door, and the congregation remains seated for a final piece of music offered by our musicians. This gives space for the worship to settle in people's bodies and hearts, a pause between the end of the formal liturgy and the invitation to engage in conversation and supper after the service. The mood can vary from lament to praise, from sorrow to celebration, but again the intention is to enable connection between worship and the whole of life.

At the conclusion of most services, those present are invited to stay on for a time of conversation and sharing. For those in the hall, this fellowship includes a simple supper of wine and cheese; for those attending online, it involves staying on for conversation. These are significant opportunities for people to share what is happening in their lives, to reflect together on responses to the liturgy, to express concern for the world and for others in the community. As is common in many contexts, this informal sharing helps people feel connected to one another and generates the relational context in which our prayer and care can deepen.

CONCLUSION

I have said already that Benedictus does not presume to offer the only template for contemplative worship. Some congregations will emerge within established denominational churches that may have authorized liturgies and protocols and less scope for innovation and change. Others will find what we have shared here unsuited for their context and culture. What we have sought to do, however, is to share not simply examples and resources, but the understanding and intention that lies behind and around these rhythms and words. Whether or not these specific liturgical forms and prayers resonate, our hope is that sharing the questions we have grappled with and choices we have made will contribute to others discerning their own call to worship in spirit and in truth.

What, however, is involved in learning to create such liturgies in the context of community? Jenny Stewart is a member of Benedictus and coordinator of our liturgy writing group. Her reflections in the next chapter share something of this process.

— 4 —

CREATING CONTEMPLATIVE LITURGY

A Reflection on Practice

Jenny Stewart

I WAS NOT RAISED a Christian. Although my father's sisters were very devout, he himself was agnostic and my Mum was a convinced atheist. I was sent to Sunday school because Mum thought it was important to learn about religion, even if you didn't believe in it. Somehow, though, the stories I learned then must have become part of me. After awful depression in my teens, I decided, possibly as an unconventional act of rebellion, to get myself confirmed as an Anglican. This, however, proved a passing phase. My husband, whom I married in my late twenties, was a convinced rationalist. Working hard in the bureaucracy and in academia, I tried hard to develop a professional persona.

Yet somehow the spiritual energy I needed to survive kept draining away. I tried Buddhism and took refuge with a local teacher, but despite the compelling nature of the teachings, I did not quite fit in with the culture. I decided, not for the first time, that I had no talent for organized religion. It was not until much later in life that I realized there was, for me, no alternative to Christianity. As with many who come to this realization, the change happened as the result of life circumstances—my marriage had fallen apart, leaving no exit path, and in 2010 my mother, still with unfinished emotional business all around her, died of cancer. This time, though, I was lucky. When I felt I had no other options, I simply walked into the conventional Anglican church down the road and was accepted as I had never been before. I cannot stress too strongly how important that first welcome is. I am not sure I would have persisted without it. But there was a further stage to go. It is said that when the student is ready, the teacher appears. I heard Sarah interviewed on the radio, and realized that a woman theologian actually lived in my city and, what's more, had started an independent church. And so I came to Benedictus, which from the start struck me as something different, truly a breath of fresh air. Benedictus did not wall you in; it opened up possibilities for a new kind of spiritual wondering. I have been wondering and growing, and growing and wondering, ever since.

The first Benedictus group I joined was Theology Reading Group, where I started to understand what it means to try to reason about faith. As a former academic, I found this introduction invaluable. Theology seemed to me a very special discipline, based on belief, but also constructing analytical pathways that needed to be absorbed if I wanted to make progress in my own practice. I asked lots of questions! Also, as a writer, I was attracted to the idea of using this knowledge, without trying to become a theologian, to express myself spiritually. So it was that when I saw the Liturgy Group was looking for members, I made contact. While I was familiar with writing intercessory prayers in a traditional Anglican context, Benedictus offered the privilege and responsibility of going further, crafting the words for an entire service—not, I hasten to add, every week, but for a number of weeks during the year.

This began a journey that has involved lots of discovery and a good deal of frustration, learning to accept, even welcome, critical feedback, all with the aim of creating rhythms and words in service of the worship of the community, words that connect feeling and thinking and that open space for deep listening and receptivity to the divine.

CRAFTING CONTEMPLATIVE LITURGY

Initially, I must confess, apart from the music, I paid little attention to the Benedictus liturgies. For me, they bookended the reflection, which was my main reason for being there. Over time, however, my perspective changed. As I now see it, liturgies structure our formal relationship with the world of the Spirit. But they take time to do their work. I am sure I have been changed by listening and responding to them through the seasons, through the years. I have grown into them and they into me.

Liturgies, as I understand it, are prayers—prayers that are meant to resound collectively. As the words resonate, they should help to bring us together. Many liturgies do this by being standardized, and traditional liturgies can offer real comfort and inspiration. The most beautiful prayers, such as the Anglican collects, stay in the mind because they have been distilled many times over. For many, however, too much tradition can be a deterrent; and for others, the familiarity of repetition has bred a kind of staleness. Benedictus takes a different approach. The components are standardized, but the content is not. As a contemplative church, it privileges silence, and this brings an added dimension. It raises the question of the place of words, music, and vocal prayer in relation to the silence.

The Benedictus Liturgy Group has focused on writing for defined seasons of the liturgical year—Advent, Lent, and the Season of Creation—though we have also contributed to services at other times, such as Dark Night of the Season and the Harvest Festival. The theme for each service focuses attention. I have found that discerning and working with these seasonal themes has brought me closer to the foundational texts. No matter how many times you read particular passages from the Bible, something new will always strike you. If there were just one meaning, fixed and irrevocable, we would not keep going back to it, but these are texts that are constantly revealing their depths. How, then, do we go about the process of crafting new liturgies?

Like many multifaceted activities, writing liturgy is best done with others, but not too many others! The Benedictus Liturgy Group has three core members. Over time we have grown to understand each other's particular outlooks and skills. We welcome new members, but we have found that introducing new people gradually to the work of the group, initially by having them audit our sessions, works better than expecting usable drafts from the outset. Writing with friends and colleagues has a number of advantages—we workshop our words with each other before sending our drafts to Sarah. As we refine what we have written, if the sense is still not clear, we ask each other, what do you mean by this? Can you make this clearer? Very often, we find that less is more. Too many words slow down the pace, or distract the listener.

Every word of liturgy is implicit theology. To create liturgies responsibly means being aware of your own theological vision and understanding, and being conscious of how ways of naming or communicating God affect the community as a whole. Within a group, theological understanding will differ from person to person, and, over time, perspectives can change within each one of us. While writing liturgies we need to be alert to how people in the congregation may think and feel, but it also seems to me we should not be afraid to take something of a poetic punt. Maggie Ross's description of liturgy as "ritualized wilderness"[1] resonates with me, and it inspires some of my prayers.

> God of the still, small voice,
> we who are conflicted by
> needs, hopes, dreams, and dreads
> often cannot hear you.
> Have mercy on us.
> Help us recognize the God-melody
> in tune with our human heart-beat. **Amen.**

---

1. Ross, *Writing the Icon*, 44.

Creating Contemplative Liturgy

In chapter 3, Sarah has described how each element of the liturgy has a particular function within the overall context of the service. The opening responses situate listeners and bring the service into focus. The gathering prayer or collect, as its name implies, is a prayer of bringing together, of "collecting" and gathering ourselves. Because Benedictus draws people from both northern and southern hemispheres into its worshiping life, we often need to be mindful of the potential for seasonal references or metaphors to unintentionally exclude or fail to gather the whole congregation. This gathering prayer, written for Dark Night of the Season, seeks to encompass all of us.

> We come in summer sun and
> winter darkness;
>
> **lives knit together,**
> **across a spinning earth.**
>
> Help us to find the stillness
> at the center,
>
> **and from it know**
> **your promise of rebirth.**

Closing responses sum up the feeling or intention of the service. They name the terrain we have covered and orient us towards next steps.

> God be the call
> **to which we answer.**
>
> God be the desire
> **through which we love.**
>
> God be the imagination
> **inspiring our vision.**
>
> God be the reconciliation
> **drawing us together.**

The blessing is the denouement, the beautiful words of assurance and continuity spoken over the congregation by the celebrant.

> God shine within us, give us hope;
> God shine among us, give us joy;
> God shine in the world, guide our steps.
> And the blessing of God, who calls us out of darkness,
> be with us all, this day and for evermore. **Amen.**

In our group, we all find the most difficult prayers to write are the intercessory prayers. From speaking with those who lead intercessions in mainstream churches, I know this hesitancy is widespread. For these prayers, the invocation and the relationship it implies are always important. How do we understand God? How do we rightly address God? Some members of the congregation have grown up with punitive or otherwise distorted images of God; you risk triggering old, uncomfortable, even traumatic associations if you orient the words the wrong way. Conversely, choosing words that bring God closer, inclusive rather than exclusive, and even daring to argue with God in our prayer, help communicate a different theology.

> Creator God
> It's good that we can argue with you.
> How else to know your will?
> We peer inside the atom
> and find worlds within worlds.
> We look outwards, and find worlds beyond worlds.
> What were you thinking when you made us?
> The more we discover, the further we have to go.
> **May all our perplexities be pathways to you.**

THE PROCESS

So, having formed a liturgy team, how to proceed? Someone needs to coordinate the work and take responsibility for communicating within the group and with the service leader about the readings and emerging themes. I draw up a table for the sequence of liturgies we will be writing so we can keep track of what we have agreed. Ahead of writing each week's liturgy, we decide among the group which prayer we will undertake to contribute. This is useful, as the types of prayer have their own resonance and become more familiar over time. As I do my own preparation, I read the scriptural passage several times, letting it settle within me. Regular meditation, however patchy, offers an anchor point for steadying the mind, letting the mind descend to the heart. As we bring our drafts together, we find that some of the themes we have explored seem to overlap. This is not a problem in itself because it means these are strong messages that will resonate with others. Nevertheless, as we listen and respond to each other, a slight shift of perspective may bring out a new or more extensive meaning. I think you must like words to be a liturgist, but you certainly don't need to be an accomplished or experienced writer. Liturgy writing is its own skill, one that takes time and patience to develop. How do we develop this skill? Here I share four elements that have been significant for me.

First, reading. If you want to write spiritually, you need to read. Steep yourself in writing that inspires. There are many authors, whether poets, mystics, or theologians, who provide prompts and inspiration. My own favorites are the Sufi poet Rumi, the visionary Meister Eckhart, and, from more recent times, poet Mary Oliver and liturgist Janet Morley. There is also a rich literature relating to contemplation, from the writing of Laurence Freeman and John Main to Cynthia Bourgeault, Richard Rohr, and Martin Laird.

Second, listening to the heart. This is more difficult to describe. For me it is something like an interaction between word and emotion, between the readings, theme, and personal experience. Each season has its own climate or atmosphere. Lent evokes notions of journeying and sacrifice; Pentecost is a time of revelation and inspiration. There is something about dwelling with the Scripture and unfolding the meaning of a season in prayer and reflection that brings us to the inside of its liturgical movement and its potential gift for the community. This is the depth dimension we seek to bring to our creation of new liturgy.

Third, being realistic. As with most writing, it is better to get material down, even if it does not seem to work, than to be so self-critical that you cannot get started, or you become discouraged when you reread what you have written. Even if you think you have nailed it, be prepared to revise or even rethink what you have written.

Finally, giving and accepting criticism. This may be the hardest skill of all to develop. Suggestions for change or revision, no matter how delicately expressed, can make us all feel a little put out. Defensiveness is a natural reaction. This is why it is important for the group to have allocated adequate time for each member to consider and revise what they have written, and why contemplative practice is integral to the process. As we are less identified with our own "performance," we gradually become more open to this kind of engagement. No matter how diligent you are, or how much experience you accumulate, you will not always hit the mark. Perfection is not attainable. But consensus within the group has its own power to reassure. I find the trick as a liturgist is to imagine myself as a channel, from within to without and from without to within. Ultimately, the measure of the liturgy is the extent to which it means something to the congregation and serves the prayer of the whole.

When we have contributed a liturgy, Benedictus service sheets credit the members of the group by name, but there is no attribution for individual prayers. In any case, as the words are said or listened to, they become the prayers of the congregation and from there (I imagine) pass into the general world of worship. When I reread them now, I recognize some as "mine," but many have become genuinely communal, in the sense that they reflect the collective spirit of the Liturgy Group and, beyond that, the collective spirit of the community for whom they were written.

CONCLUSION

Every contemplative community has a different history, different character, different values, different expectations. Because of this diversity, the liturgy can never be standardized. The words that will land, even when the same or similar themes are being explored, will be different from one church to the next.

As for me, even after several years of practice, I have found that liturgy writing is hard work. I also know that, every time I take part, my personal theology moves on a bit. And in imagining a voice that will resonate with others, I feel the full importance of community—and understand more of why Paul wrote all those letters! Creating contemplative liturgy in and for community is indeed a responsibility. It is also a privilege to be entrusted with this work on behalf of the whole, one whose joys I celebrate and commend.

— 5 —

INTEGRATING WORSHIP

IN A RANGE OF ways, we have emphasized the significance of integrity in our contemplative worship. By "integrity" we mean a sense of wholeness or congruence *between* the liturgy and the life of the community and the wider world, as well as the integration *within* the liturgy of word, music, and silence. In this final chapter, we share two complete liturgies, including the reflection, so as to offer a taste of the Benedictus service as a whole. In practice, participants in a Benedictus service never receive the full text of the liturgy like this; the acknowledgment of country, the Scripture reading, reflection, and Eucharistic preface are not included in our service sheet as text but offered to be heard. Here, however, we have set out the whole script, except for the words of the songs.

These printed pages cannot, of course, convey the felt experience of participating with others at a given moment in time. They cannot represent the external conditions of darkness or light, warmth or cold, nor the inner weather of the community and individuals within it. Nor can we generate here the effect of being bodily present as we cocreate worship, hearing and singing the music, sharing the silence and the spoken responses. Yet, however pale a reflection of the lived reality these printed pages might be, once again we hope they communicate something that may be useful for other contexts.

Integrating Worship

As you engage with and enter these liturgies, you may find it helpful to prepare yourself as if for a time of worship. You might like to clear some inner and outer space, allowing a few minutes of silence, attending to your physical environment and bodily posture, before entering in. It will be helpful to attend to the pace of your engagement with these liturgies, allowing pauses between the elements as would happen in a live service. This might include allowing a significant space between the Scripture reading and reflection, and then between the reflection and meditation. It may also be helpful to read the responses aloud as if you were participating in their answering movement. A liturgy is not so much to be understood as embodied, and we encourage readers to approach the chapter in this spirit.

Evening Liturgy: Dark Night of the Season

The first liturgy offered here is for a non-Eucharistic service. The theme is Dark Night of the Season, and this liturgy was created for our annual midwinter service. It was also the final service in a four-week preaching series called "The Word of the Lord," in which we were exploring what it means to recognize Jesus as the incarnation of God's word, connecting this Gospel theme with the notion of Wisdom in the Hebrew Scriptures.

From Impasse to Wisdom
Dark Night of the Season

Welcome

Opening Responses

When we cannot see the way ahead,
lighten our path.

When we are in thrall to dark thoughts and ways,
enlighten our minds.

When we desire what is not love,
set our hearts on fire for you.

God of the darkness and the light,
call us forth into what is good
and right and true.

Acknowledging Country

We remember the land on which we meet. We acknowledge the Ngunnawal people as traditional custodians of this piece of God's good creation. We acknowledge the way Aboriginal peoples' connection to country nurtures body, mind, and spirit and sustains the life and well-being of creatures. The elders teach that the land is not ours to own, but a gift to care for and delight in. If we listen deeply, we may hear in the life of the world the calling of the eternal Spirit.

Gathering Prayer

God of darkness
of velvet black and gritty nights.
Help us to see beauty in nuance.
We ask for hearts that beat
to love in every season.
You who spoke and called the light.
Amen.

Song

Reading

Let us listen for the Word of God. *(Silence is kept.)*

Integrating Worship

A reading from Matthew 13:51–58

> "Have you understood all this?" They answered, "Yes." And he said to them, "Therefore every scribe who has been trained for the kingdom of heaven is like the master of a household who brings out of his treasure what is new and what is old." When Jesus had finished these parables, he left that place.
>
> He came to his home town and began to teach the people in their synagogue, so that they were astounded and said, "Where did this man get this wisdom and these deeds of power? Is not this the carpenter's son? Is not his mother called Mary? And are not his brothers James and Joseph and Simon and Judas? And are not all his sisters with us? Where then did this man get all this?" And they took offence at him. But Jesus said to them, "Prophets are not without honor except in their own country and in their own house." And he did not do many deeds of power there, because of their unbelief.

Reflection

"Have you understood all this?" Jesus asked his disciples. "They answered: 'Yes'" (Matt 13:51).

I wonder about the tone of that "yes." Was it "yes!" as in "absolutely," "of course," "yep—we've followed," "we're with you," "let's move on" . . . or was it "ye-e-e-es" as in, "sort of," "we think so," "it's probably not gonna get much clearer"? As Matthew portrays events, Jesus poses this question after a fairly solid run of parables about the kingdom of heaven, in which he draws on analogies ranging from treasure hidden in a field, to a merchant in search of fine pearls, to a net catching fish both good and bad, some of which are tossed into the furnace of fire. Have you understood all this? "Well, more or less . . ."

Over the past month, we've been exploring the ways in which the Jesus of Matthew's Gospel explicitly identifies himself with the figure of divine Wisdom, Wisdom with a capital "W." In the wisdom literature of the Hebrew Bible, Wisdom is personified as the active, creative, loving intelligence present *with* God, present *as* God, at the foundation of the world. Think of Wisdom's speech in the book of Proverbs: "When God established the heavens, I was there, when he drew a circle on the face of the deep, when he made firm the skies above . . . then I was beside him, like a master worker, and I was daily his delight, rejoicing before him always, rejoicing in his inhabited world and delighting in the human race" (Prov 8:27–31). Jesus' astonishing claim is that *he* is this Wisdom's embodied presence. He is Wisdom's power and truth at work *within* the life of the world. "Wisdom is vindicated by her deeds," Jesus has said (Matt 11:19), when accounting for his actions; and "I will proclaim what has been hidden from the foundation of the world" (Matt 13:35).

And yet, paradoxically, the wisdom of Jesus, the Wisdom Jesus *is*, struggles to make itself known and to communicate its gift. Most of those around him do not recognize him, and cannot understand what he says and does. Jesus diagnoses their incomprehension in terms of quasi-culpable incapacity: they have ears but do not hear, he says, eyes but do not see, and their heart has grown dull (Matt 13:15). Again and again, he tries to wake them up, to draw them into a fuller way of knowing. Thus, his use of parables, metaphors, similes, unexpected juxtapositions, and unconventional acts. It's as if he wants to jolt his hearers into new possibilities for understanding and for being, by confounding their expectations, bringing them to the limits of their habituated way of seeing and knowing.

So how's that been working for him? You might recall that our series on Wisdom began at chapter 11 of Matthew's Gospel, verse 1: "Now when Jesus had finished instructing his twelve disciples, he went on from there to teach and proclaim his message in their cities." As we've just heard, this block of teaching concludes with more or less the same formula: "When Jesus had finished these parables, he left that place" (Matt 13:53). Job done. Except . . . what's the first thing that happens in the next chapter of his ministry? He goes to his hometown, he begins to teach in the synagogue, and—all over again—people refuse to hear him. "Where did this man get this wisdom and these deeds of power? Is not this the

Integrating Worship

carpenter's son?" Don't we know his family? Who does he think he is? "And they took offence at him."

In the passage we read four weeks ago, Jesus had responded to questions concerning his identity by pointing to his deeds: the blind receiving their sight, the lame walking, the lepers being cleansed. "And," he'd said, "blessed is anyone who takes no offense at me" (Matt 11:6). Four weeks and two Gospel chapters later, and they're offended yet again. Has anyone learned anything? Or is Jesus simply up against a brick wall in human being? A lack of hospitality to truth, mercy, solidarity? And if so, how is Wisdom ever to break through, to break in, so as to free and heal a world turned in on itself, ensnarled by petty power plays, lack of awareness, futile game-playing, and the forces of de-creation? Seemingly, things in the Gospel are at an impasse[1]: "He did not do many deeds of power there, because of their unbelief" (13:58).

As I've sat with this passage, one of the things that strikes me is the way in which Jesus and his disciples seem to be in a kind of parallel process. In order to convey the fullness of God's way, Jesus wants to liberate his hearers from some of their default ways of being and knowing, their habits of fear, aggression, acquisition. This involves the use of parables—stories that help us see ourselves differently—but there's more to it than that. He consistently draws those who want to learn from him past self-reliance and conventional systems of goodness, past their capacity to control or make sense of their lives in the old terms. The disciples are called from their fishing nets, from their families, from their respectable places in the synagogue, from beyond the lives they've known. For them, the water is deep and getting deeper.

But (and this is the parallel process), Jesus isn't communicating God's way from a safe distance, depositing it from on high. Rather, he embodies it right in the midst of them, himself letting go the security of anonymity and family life, himself increasingly misunderstood and threatened. In the verses immediately following our passage, Jesus receives news of the beheading of John the Baptist by

---

1. The notion of "impasse" comes from Fitzgerald, "Impasse and Dark Night."

King Herod. Matthew writes, "Now when Jesus heard this, he withdrew from there in a boat to a deserted place by himself" (14:13). The water is deep and getting deeper. It's as if Jesus and his disciples are being drawn into the necessity of ever-deepening faith, ever-deepening reliance on the One who beckons, through the narrowing and darkening, even the felt sense of losing their way.

The great sixteenth-century Spanish mystic John of the Cross spoke of the "dark night of the soul" as intrinsic to the process of spiritual maturing.[2] It's in this undergoing, John says, that the meaning of God is truly learned and human being is truly transformed. Why? Because it's only by losing our way, losing ourselves, being dispossessed of all that is false in us, self-centered, and self-reliant, that we may receive the fullness of God and so begin to live *from* gift, *at* peace, and *in* abundance. This is the truth Jesus comes to share, and it cannot be made known just by talking about it. He can communicate it and enable us to entrust ourselves to it, only by living it himself. This is why the gospel insists that ultimately the Wisdom of God is revealed by Jesus' death on a cross and the empty tomb. As Rowan Williams puts it, it's only by undergoing failure, rejection, and death that Jesus can "at last 'say' what is to be said; as if the silence of his dying is the only rhetoric for his gospel."[3]

And here's the difficult truth of discipleship. For us, to learn from him, to come to live with him from the same source, means undergoing the same dispossession, the same yielding, so to discover for ourselves that, as Williams writes, "failure and loss do not mean final destruction or emptiness. Meaning, promise, the future, the possibility of continuing to live in freedom and in the resource to love—all these are 'held' in the being of God."[4] This is the wisdom Jesus comes to teach, "the message of the cross," which, as St. Paul admits, looks to us like foolishness but is in fact "the power of God and the wisdom of God" (1 Cor 1:18, 24).

---

2. John of the Cross, *Ascent*, 46.
3. Williams, *On Christian Theology*, 270.
4. Williams, *On Christian Theology*, 270.

So what does this mean for our lives, here and now? Let me conclude with two things. The concept of the dark night can sound romantic, glamorous even. But the lived experience is anything but. Many things can lead us past the point where we can make sense of our lives on our old terms, past the illusion that we can sustain our goodness and meaning for ourselves. Sometimes prayer itself leads us into the darkness, as our old religious feeling dries up and becomes empty. We may undergo an erosion of faith, the slow collapse of hopes, the creeping despair of diminishing capacities and approaching mortality. Sometimes a dark night, a felt sense of impasse, loss, confusion, and despair, is precipitated by grief or illness, by powerlessness in the face of injustice, or by experiences of entrapment and dysfunction. Many of you, many of your loved ones, are undergoing such things. And there's a sense in which all of us are undergoing what some have called a global dark night as the environmental crisis confronts us with the catastrophic impacts of ways of knowing and being that, even now, we seem unable to give up or transform. In a dark night, there is suffering, and there's no guarantee we'll come through it expanded, rather than diminished, destroyed.

And this leads me to the second thing. If we *are* to come through the night, if the experience of impasse, death, loss, and emptiness is actually to lead us into a more truthful, compassionate, God-given way of being in the world, then what matters is how we live it. Carmelite theologian Constance Fitzgerald speaks of the necessity of yielding in the right way, responding *with full consciousness* of one's suffering . . . yet daring to believe that new possibilities, beyond immediate vision, can be given.[5] This doesn't mean denying the reality of grief and destruction, the waste of life. It doesn't mean suppressing lament, anguish, and pain. But it does mean continuing to be open, as best we can, to the promise of God: even when we don't feel it, when we don't and can't believe it, even when we lose what we hold most dear. And it means continuing to align our being and action, as best we can, in accordance with that promise—open-hearted, self-giving, compassionate, truthful.

5. Fitzgerald, "Impasse and Dark Night."

This isn't easy in the middle of the night. Jesus himself didn't find it so. But the Wisdom he lives and dies to share is that there is "an eternal presence, an agency and intelligence wholly committed to who we are and who we shall become," and that it is possible for us to live "consistently, courageously" in its light and from its love, for the healing of the world.[6]

"Have you understood all this?" Jesus asks his disciples. Have you understood?

Meditation

Prayers

You who know the secrets of our hearts,
the treasure buried deep, the fears we
cannot name, be present to and with us.
**In the light of your Wisdom,
teach us to live.** *(Chant)*

You who know the suffering of our world,
the doubts that corrode, the sickness that
exhausts, the confusion that threatens,
the abuses of power and the terrors of
death, be present to and with us.
**In the light of your Wisdom,
teach us to live.** *(Chant)*

You who know the pain of rejection and
misunderstanding, the helplessness to
transform those who will not hear, and the
grief at willful destruction, be present to
and with us and our broken world.
**In the light of your Wisdom,
may we learn to live.** *(Chant)*

---

6. Williams, *Being Disciples*, 34.

Integrating Worship

Song

Closing Responses

We seek your face,
beyond the darkness.

We seek your light,
beyond what blinds us.

We seek your ways,
beyond our distractions.

We seek your transforming love,
beyond our resistance.

**Clothe us in your light
that we may grow into your likeness.**

Blessing

Through the ease of summer
and the chill of winter,
through our fallow seasons
and our fruitful ones

May we find the faith to keep walking
When nights are long and the stars dim.

And may the blessing of God,
who brought forth light and went into darkness,
be among us and remain with us.
Amen.

HOLY COMMUNION: A VIRGIN SHALL CONCEIVE

The second whole liturgy we offer is a Eucharistic liturgy from Advent. This service comes from the end of 2020, the first year of the COVID-19 pandemic. It was part of a series called "Advent in and as a Time of Crisis." We were seeking to connect the sense of crisis that suffuses the liturgical season of Advent with the sense of crisis or turning that suffused the general discourse at that time in relation to the possibilities of a post-COVID recovery. It was also our final Benedictus service before Christmas.

A VIRGIN SHALL CONCEIVE
FOURTH WEEK OF ADVENT

Welcome

Opening Responses

The most Holy God
favored Mary,
and through her child,
befriends us all.

"Do not be afraid."
God comes to us
and is here among us,
making possible the impossible.

As God comes again
this Advent season,
may we embrace God's call,
beyond fear and resistance,
saying with Mary:
"Here I am. Let it be with me
according to your word."

Integrating Worship

Acknowledging Country

We remember the land on which we meet. We acknowledge the Ngunnawal people as traditional custodians of this piece of God's good creation. We acknowledge the way Aboriginal peoples' connection to country nurtures body, mind, and spirit and sustains the life and well-being of creatures. The elders teach that the land is not ours to own, but a gift to care for and delight in. If we listen deeply, we may hear in the life of the world the calling of the eternal Spirit.

Gathering Prayer

We struggle so hard to know who we are,
searching for an identity to hold us together.
Then we become aware of someone greater.
We start to dream of who we might become.

Pay attention, now.
Something is about to happen.

Song

Reading

Let us listen for the Word of God. *(Silence is kept.)*

A reading from Luke 1:26–38

> In the sixth month the angel Gabriel was sent by God to a town in Galilee called Nazareth, to a virgin engaged to a man whose name was Joseph, of the house of David. The virgin's name was Mary. And he came to her and said, "Greetings, favored one! The Lord is with you." But she was much perplexed by his words and pondered what sort of greeting this might be. The angel said to her, "Do not be afraid, Mary, for you have found favor with God. And now, you will conceive in your womb and bear a

son, and you will name him Jesus. He will be great, and will be called the Son of the Most High, and the Lord God will give to him the throne of his ancestor David. He will reign over the house of Jacob for ever, and of his kingdom there will be no end." Mary said to the angel, "How can this be, since I am a virgin?" The angel said to her, "The Holy Spirit will come upon you, and the power of the Most High will overshadow you; therefore the child to be born will be holy; he will be called Son of God. And now, your relative Elizabeth in her old age has also conceived a son; and this is the sixth month for her who was said to be barren. For nothing will be impossible with God." Then Mary said, "Here am I, the servant of the Lord; let it be with me according to your word." Then the angel departed from her.

Reflection

We've been engaging this season of Advent in and as a time of crisis. And one of the key underlying crises of our time involves a loss of confidence in the institutions of civil society, in the media and politics, even democracy itself. This is a complex story—and the past year in Australia has shown that confidence can be regained when institutions show themselves to be trustworthy, as has happened by and large in the authorities' response to the pandemic here. At the same time, trust remains fragile. And while there continue to be revelations of such things as the corrupt use of public funds, the disproportionate impact of lobbying and cronyism on public policy, and the systemic punishment of poverty and vulnerability, distrust and a sense of powerlessness among citizens grows, with all the dangers that entails.

For when people suspect they're being played, there's fruitful ground for conspiracy theories to take hold, for a lived sense of a common cause to dwindle, and for anger, frustration and blame to escalate. In some cases, this anger is then mobilized and misdirected towards the "other," the "outsider," or even towards authorities who are actually seeking to do the right thing. I'm thinking, for example, of those protesting lockdowns or refusing to wear masks in the name of their so-called "right" to freedom. Public discourse and social media are often polarized and weaponized, while those attempting nuanced engagement with complexity are squeezed out and silenced.

Recently, through the World Community for Christian Meditation, I was involved in a conversation about such matters with Herman van Rompuy. Van Rompuy is a Belgian politician who served as prime minister there from 2008 to 2009 and was later the first permanent president of the European Council (2010–2014). He talked about the polarizing of politics and the rise of populism that threatens many societies at their root. He touched on some of the underlying social causes I've just mentioned, but he also raised the question of the spiritual dimension of this crisis. "Why," he asked, "is there so much inner dissatisfaction, which is then politically translated into aggression?"[7] Does it have to do with the hyper-competitiveness of our society? Is it connected with excessive individualism, which brings disconnection from others and lack of empathy? Or, he asked, does it have to do with the superficiality of much of our life—a life focused on activity and pleasure-seeking with little listening, self-interrogation, or recognition of our fundamental dependency? Are we suffering collectively, he wondered, from the lack of interiority as a counterforce against anger and impatience? "Living together," he said, "is based on the sharing of values and of common destiny, but those values must also have an inner foundation if they are to withstand storms.... They need to be interior[ized]."[8]

Well—I'm aware this seems a long way from the angel Gabriel visiting a virgin whose name was Mary, but I was reminded of this conversation by our text. For Mary has traditionally been a symbol of radical and fruitful interiority. And I'm interested in what she offers in relation to this spiritual crisis of our culture. In particular, I want to explore what might be gleaned from the significance of Mary's virginity in the Christmas story.

7. Van Rompuy et al., "Contemplative Conscious Mind," 29:27
8. Van Rompuy et al., "Contemplative Conscious Mind," 36:11.

This may seem an unpromising and, indeed, politically incorrect place to start. So here's what I think the story's insistence on her virginity is not about. It's not essentially about the mechanics of Jesus' conception. At least, not in an obvious biological sense. In the scriptural imagination, the virginity of Mary, like the barrenness of Sarah and Hannah and Elizabeth, is a sign that what's being given and what is to happen in and through this child of promise is God's doing, not ours. Again and again, in the story of Israel, where the way (the womb) had seemed closed, where impossibility had reigned, God remains free to act so as to create new life. The overshadowing of Mary by the Holy Spirit is thus meant to evoke not a creepy sense of male domination, but the hovering of the Spirit over the waters at the creation of the world itself. "Creation occurs," writes theologian Ben Myers, "when the Spirit of God broods over the formless abyss and brings forth life out of nothing."[9]

Now I know this imagery has been taken up by our tradition in troubling ways. When combined with Aristotelian biology and a vision of God as male, for example, it's contributed to an understanding of women as providing only "formless matter" in procreation, with all the form and animating energy coming from the male. When combined with gnostic teaching on the evils of the flesh, Mary's "virginity" has contributed to a centuries-long ambivalence in Christianity about sexuality and the body, and about women's sexuality and bodies especially. As feminist critics have pointed out, in the hands of a patriarchal church, Mary became the measure by which all other women were predestined to fail.[10] For what real woman could live as both virgin and mother? In the light of this oppressive and distorting history, retrieving her meaning for us is quite a task.

Nevertheless, what I love about the figure of Mary is that though she gives herself without remainder to what God will do in and through her, she's not some passive vessel. She is always actively engaged—inquiring, consenting, reflecting on meaning,

---

9. Myers, *Apostles' Creed*, 43.
10. See, for example, Warner, *Alone of All Her Sex*.

striving to integrate her experience with her understanding. In her encounter with the angel, she is said to be much perplexed and to have pondered what sort of greeting this might be. After Jesus' birth, when the shepherds visit the holy family in the stable and report what they'd been told of the child by angels, Mary is said to have "treasured all these words and pondered them in her heart" (Luke 2:19). And again, some years later, when the child Jesus frightens his parents by staying behind in Jerusalem after a festival, explaining that he "must be at his Father's house [the temple]," Luke writes that "they did not understand what he said to them" but that "his mother treasured all these things in her heart" (Luke 2:51).

Mary, in other words, is depicted as having a rich inner life, a reflective capacity, an interiority. In medieval iconography she is often portrayed in an enclosed garden, solitary, reading a book (maybe that's why I like her!). And I wonder if it's this that constitutes the deep meaning of her virginity. Because although she's humble and available, receptive and other-centered, she's never colonized or determined by events. The early church theologian Gregory of Nyssa wrote a treatise called "On Virginity," in which he understands virginity essentially as incorruptibility—a state of being to which the married as well as the celibate must aspire.[11] Incorruptibility in the sense of healthy detachment, nonattachment, purity of heart. Mary is not swayed by what people think of her; she doesn't grasp at power or influence; she remains self-possessed even as she is dispossessed, being and becoming herself in relation to God, more and more fully integrated over the years.

John Main wrote that to our era, in need of rediscovering "an inner life that has been largely dissipated in materialistic systems of thought and of society... Mary is above all the symbol of a rich, healthy and creative interiority."[12] This is the condition of her conceiving God's word, God's life, and bringing it to birth bodily; it's the condition of her becoming capable of bearing what she must

---

11. Gregory of Nyssa, "On Virginity," 553. See also the editor's preface to "On Virginity," 536.

12. Main, *Community of Love*, 164.

bear at the foot of her son's cross. And John Main goes on: "the most powerful aspect of her meaning for people today . . . is the need for a true inner harmony. . . . She shows the need for the resolution of the dissonant faculties in us, the transcendence of our sense of duality in relation to ourself and to God, the integration of *Yin* and *Yang*, the concentration of our spirit upon the source of our being."[13]

I began by citing Herman van Rompuy's wondering if the polarization of our society, the violent tone of so much public discourse and social media is significantly to do with a lack of interiority, the lack of an inner foundation or integration "as a counterforce against anger and impatience." I know it's a cop out to personalize and spiritualize all social ills—to think that frustration at injustice or disempowerment can be cured merely by exhorting people to deepen their inner life. But equally, I think it's deluded to imagine that the crisis of our culture can be healed purely by social reform. We can, as people and as societies, get into habits of reactivity, impatience, mercilessness. We can give ourselves permission always to blame someone else for our behavior, rather than doing the inner work necessary to integrate and transform our pain, our limits and shadow. We can be immature, and a society that offers no real context for spiritual formation and growth is bound to be. Van Rompuy's insight is, I think, that a widespread lack of interiority, of spiritual maturity, increases people's susceptibility to being overtaken by anger, hatred and fear. And this, in turn, profoundly increases our vulnerability to manipulation, to being exploited and persuaded by cynics and tyrants to conspire in our own and others' diminishment.

As has been said by many, this year has crystallized the crises facing our world. Much is being written about the need to build back better. But there is a spiritual dimension to this crisis and the conditions for a transformative recovery that is in grave danger of being neglected. At the turning of the age, in the New Testament's understanding, it was a virgin who conceived and bore God's son, God's meaning on earth. Someone who was recollected and pure

13. Main, *Community of Love*, 172.

of heart, integrated and so interiorly fruitful. The early Christian fathers and mothers understood Mary as a model for their own pilgrimage and for the vocation of the church itself. "In Mary they saw the reflection, indeed the ideal, of their own experience . . . because they knew that every Christian, every responsive heart, is called to bring Jesus to birth within him or her."[14] This is our vocation too, as persons and as a community, for the love of the whole. "So God imparts to human hearts / the blessings of his heaven. / No ear may hear his coming; / but in this world of sin, / where meek souls will receive him, still / the dear Christ enters in."[15] A blessed and holy Christmas to you all.

Ponder These Things

We are all in need of angels.
Will we know them when we see them?
They come in different guises—
old, young; rich, poor; shining, dull.
They may not announce themselves.
They can be quite discreet.
If we notice them,
we may find they give us aid,
or ask us questions.
Sometimes, as in the Holy Land long ago,
they announce a new story.
Bright wings, dark sky, distant star.

A time of silent reflection . . .

Prayer of Consecration

God is here.
God's Spirit is with us.

---

14. Main, *Community of Love*, 165.
15. Brooks, "O Little Town of Bethlehem," lines 19-24.

Pools of Grace

We lift up our hearts,
that we may praise God.

Let us give thanks to the God of grace.
It is right to give our thanks and praise.

Your table is set and your welcome warm,
for your love knows no bounds.
From your communing life, you long for us,
that we may be one with you,
that we may treat each other well,
and live justly and in peace.

In Christ Jesus, you came to us
and gave yourself for us, that we may learn
that nothing can separate us from your love:
neither trials nor distress,
neither sickness nor fear,
neither hatred nor death.

Therefore, with the whole creation and
all the company of heaven we praise you, saying:

Holy, holy, holy,
God whose power is love.
Heaven and earth are full of your glory.
Hosanna in the highest.
Blessed is the One who comes in God's Name.
Hosanna in the highest.

For even on the night he was betrayed, Jesus ministered to his disciples
—to Judas who would betray him, Peter who would deny him,
and to all he would leave, bewildered and sorrowing.

He took bread, and giving you thanks,
he broke it and gave it to them saying,
"Take, eat, this is my body, given for you."

After supper he took the cup, and again giving thanks,
he gave it to his disciples saying, "Drink from this, all of you.
This is my blood of the new covenant."

He bid them remember this night,
and so to live by the kindly gifts of God,
that all may be one.

Let us proclaim the mystery of faith:
Christ has died,
Christ is risen,
Christ will come again.
Gracious God, send now your Holy Spirit upon us and on these gifts of bread and wine, that we may know Christ's presence, real and true, and be his faithful followers, bearing your love for our world. **Amen.**

The Lord's Prayer

(a paraphrase)

Loving source of our life, God of us all,
reverenced may you be,
may your justice come,
your will for the world be realized.
Give us this day our daily bread.
Free us from that which binds us,
as we become those
who unbind others.
Do not let our suffering overcome us,
and save us from the power of destruction.

**For you are ever present and your love is true,
now and forever. Amen.**

Communion

Meditation

Song

Closing Responses

God of mercy, compassion, and grace:
Let us act as midwives to our rebirth.
Let us nurse our planet to health.
Let us face our fears with courage.
Let us renounce our need for more.
Let us abandon our desire for control.
Let us relearn simplicity and humility.
**Let us call on our better angels.
Let us live with love, in peace. Amen.**

Blessing

May this season of Advent be a blessing to you.
May you be open to annunciation.
May you be blessed by what grows within.
May you be ready to celebrate what is born.
May we bear God's coming among us. **Amen.**

CONCLUSION

In the foreword of this book, I emphasized the communal foundations of Benedictus, and I conclude by reiterating them. Public worship, congregational worship, is the work of a people. It calls on some to write prayers, responses, and reflections, and at Benedictus we are blessed by writers, poets, theologians, and the prayerful participation of those willing to learn. It calls on musicians and songwriters, on those who shift furniture and provide supper, and on those who offer welcome and notice the ones in need of a friendly word. In turn, the offering that is public worship calls *forth* all who come. It invites all present to open themselves to honest encounter with the truth of their lives and the truth of God.

I have said that of all the things religious communities do, worship is the one thing that has no parallel in other gatherings. Directing our attention to the reality we call God, invoking and addressing God, singing and praising, listening for and yielding to God, opening our lives to that which is infinitely beyond what we can control or understand—for many in the Western world this is no longer a practice they have much experience of or access to. For many, it occurs like a relic of a bygone age. Yet, contemplative congregational worship can form a gathering into a people who are becoming reconciled to God in the midst of all that contradicts Christ's gift and call. It can thereby send us out as agents of reconciliation, witnesses to the possibility of God in our time. It makes publicly available a certain kind of responsiveness to reality.

We hope that this book contributes to making visible the power of contemplative congregational worship to connect us to what is deepest and most essential for our life *in* the world and for the life *of* the world. It is a small seed. But Jesus said, "The kingdom of heaven is like a mustard seed that someone took and sowed in his field; it is the smallest of all the seeds, but when it has grown it is the greatest of shrubs and becomes a tree, so that the birds of the air come and make nests in its branches" (Matt 13:31–32). In these pages, then, may others find shelter and encouragement on the way.

BIBLIOGRAPHY

Adam, David. *Tides and Seasons: Modern Prayers in the Celtic Tradition.* London: Triangle SPCK, 1989.
Alison, James. "The Importance of Being Indifferent." In *On Being Liked*, 114–30. London: Darton Longman & Todd, 2003.
Anglican Church of Australia. *A Prayer Book for Australia.* Sydney: Broughton, 1995.
Bachelard, Sarah. *A Contemplative Christianity for Our Time.* Singapore: Meditatio, 2020.
———. *Poetica Divina: Poems to Redeem a Prose World.* Singapore: Meditatio, 2021.
Bendell, Jem. *Breaking Together: A Freedom-Loving Response to Collapse.* Bristol: Good Words, 2023.
Benedict. *Rule of St. Benedict in English.* Edited and translated by Timothy Fry et al. Collegeville, MN: Liturgical, 2016.
Benedictus Contemplative Church. "Reflections." https://benedictus.com.au/reflections/.
Bonhoeffer, Dietrich. *Ethics.* Edited by Clifford J. Green. Translated by Reinhard Krauss et al. Dietrich Bonhoeffer Works 6. Minneapolis, MN: Fortress, 2000.
Brooks, Phillips. "O Little Town of Bethlehem." *Together in Song, Australian Hymn Book II*, 316. East Melbourne: HarperCollinsReligious, 1999.
Bucko, Adam. "Sacred Activism: Not Everyone Finds God Through Silence. (Short Note No. 2)." *Contemplative Witness with Adam Bucko.* Substack, June 13, 2025. https://fatheradambucko.substack.com/p/sacred-activism-holy-preparation.
Church of the Province of New Zealand. *A New Zealand Prayer Book.* Auckland: Collins, 1989.
Cotter, Jim. *Prayer at Night: A Book for the Darkness.* Sheffield, UK: Cairns, 1991.
Fitzgerald, Constance. "Impasse and Dark Night." 1984. Institute for Communal Contemplation and Dialogue. https://iccdinstitute.org/impasse-and-dark-night/.

BIBLIOGRAPHY

Grant, Stan. *Murriyang: Song of Time*. Sydney: Bundyi, 2024.

Gregory of Nyssa. "On Virginity." In vol. 5 of *The Nicene and Post-Nicene Fathers*, Series 2, 5:536–86. Edited by Philip Schaff. 1893. 7 vols. Repr. Peabody, MA: Hendrickson, 1995. Christian Classics Ethereal Library. https://www.documentacatholicaomnia.eu/03d/0330-0395,_Gregorius_Nyssenus,_De_virginitate_[Schaff],_EN.pdf.

Hall, Douglas John. *The Cross in Our Context: Jesus and the Suffering World*. Minneapolis, MN: Fortress, 2003.

Iona Community. *Iona Abbey Worship Book*. Glasgow: Wild Goose, 2017.

John of the Cross. *Ascent of Mount Carmel*. Translated and edited by E. Allison Peers. Woodstock, ON: Devoted, 2016.

Main, John. *Community of Love*. New York: Continuum, 1999.

———. *Monastery Without Walls: The Spiritual Letters of John Main*. Norwich: Canterbury, 2006.

———. *Word into Silence: A Manual for Christian Meditation*. Norwich: Canterbury, 2006.

Mathews, Freya. *The Dao of Civilization: A Letter to China*. London: Anthem, 2023.

Maxwell, Florida Scott. *The Measure of My Days*. New York: Penguin, 1983.

Merton, Thomas. *Conjectures of a Guilty Bystander*. Tunbridge Wells, UK: Burns & Oates, 1995.

Myers, Ben. *The Apostles' Creed: A Guide to the Ancient Catechism*. Bellingham, WA: Lexham, 2018.

Ross, Maggie. *Silence: A User's Guide*. Vol. 1, *Process*. London: Darton Longman & Todd, 2014.

———. *Writing the Icon of the Heart: In Silence Beholding*. Oxford: Bible Reading Fellowship, 2011.

Rowson, Jonathan. *Metamodernity: Dispatches from a Time Between Worlds*. London: Perspectiva, 2021.

Steiner, George. *Real Presences: Is There Anything in What We Say?* London: Faber and Faber, 1989.

Sweeney, Jon M., and Mark S. Burrows. *Meister Eckhart's Book of the Heart: Meditations for the Restless Soul*. Charlottesville, VA: Hampton Roads, 2017.

Ungunmerr, Miriam Rose. *Australian Stations of the Cross*. Melbourne: Dove Communications, 1984.

———. "Dadirri: Inner Deep Listening and Quiet Still Awareness." Emmaus Productions, 2002. http://www.dadirri.org.au/wp-content/uploads/2015/03/Dadirri-Inner-Deep-Listening-M-R-Ungunmerr-Bauman-Refl1.pdf.

Van Rompuy, Herman, et al. "The Contemplative Conscious Mind: A Conversation with Herman Van Rompuy." Nov. 28, 2020. https://acontemplativepath-wccm.org/the-contemplative-conscious-mind-a-conversation-with-herman-von-rompoy/.

Bibliography

Vernon, Mark. "Spiritual Intelligence: What It Is, Why It's Needed, How It Might Return." Perspectiva, Oct. 20, 2021. https://systems-souls-society.com/spiritual-intelligence-what-it-is-why-its-needed-how-it-might-return.

Warner, Marina. *Alone of All Her Sex: The Myth and the Cult of the Virgin Mary*. London: Vintage, 1983.

Williams, Rowan. "Address to the Synod of Bishops on the New Evangelization for the Transmission of the Christian Faith." Rome, Oct. 10, 2012. https://episcopalnewsservice.org/2012/10/10/archbishop-of-canterburys-address-to-the-synod-of-bishops-in-rome/.

———. *Being Christian: Baptism, Bible, Eucharist, Prayer*. London: SPCK, 2014.

———. *Being Disciples: Essentials of Christian Life*. London: SPCK, 2016.

———. *The Edge of Words: God and the Habits of Language*. London: Bloomsbury, 2014.

———. Foreword to *Silence: A User's Guide*, vol. 1, *Process*, by Maggie Ross, ix–x. London: Darton Longman & Todd, 2014.

———. *Looking East in Winter: Contemporary Thought and the Eastern Christian Tradition*. London: Bloomsbury Continuum, 2021.

———. *On Christian Theology*. Oxford: Blackwell, 2000.

———. *Resurrection: Interpreting the Easter Gospel*. Rev. ed. Cleveland, OH: Pilgrim, 2002.

Wittgenstein, Ludwig. Letter to B. Russell, Aug. 19, 1919. In *Wittgenstein in Cambridge: Letters and Documents 1911–1951*, edited by Brian McGuinness, no. 63. Malden, MA: Blackwell, 2008. https://archive.org/stream/WittgensteinCorrespondance/Wittgenstein_in_cambridge_lettersAndDocuments1911-1951_djvu.txt.

Yunkaporta, Tyson. *Sand Talk: How Indigenous Thinking Can Save the World*. Melbourne: Text, 2019.

www.ingramcontent.com/pod-product-compliance
Lightning Source LLC
Chambersburg PA
CBHW071219160426
43196CB00012B/2350